RAGGEDY ANN AND ANDY'S
GREEN THUMB BOOK

RAGGEDY ANN AND ANDY'S GREEN THUMB BOOK

An Adventure in Growing Things— Indoors and Out

by Alix Nelson

BOBBS-MERRILL
Indianapolis / New York

Copyright 1928 Bobbs-Merrill Co., Inc.

CONTENTS

Let us start a garden, you and I.
Let us turn the soil of acquaintanceship
And in this fertile ground plant kindly thoughts,
Let us pull all weeds of envy and selfishness
And destroy them!
Let us water our garden with the dew of sympathy.
Let us keep our growing plants in the sunshine of love,
And happiness is ours; our garden is filled
With the beautiful flowers of friendship.

—FROM *Raggedy Ann's*
Wishing Pebble

CHAPTER ONE

SOME BULBS GLOW, SOME BULBS GROW

RAGGEDY ANN and Raggedy Andy were two rag dolls who belonged to a young girl named Marcella. They had red wool hair, shoe-button eyes, and great big smiles which were painted on their faces so that no matter how roughly they were played with, they were always cheerful and ready for more.

The two Raggedys lived in Marcella's room with lots of other dolls: Henny, the Dutch doll who wore wooden shoes and said "Mamma" whenever he was tipped backward and forward; Uncle Clem, a very nice man doll with a yarn moustache and a plaid kilt; an Indian brave with a fine feather headdress; and a shiny tin soldier with a helmet and gun. There was also a French doll with a beautiful dress and hat, a stuffed camel with baggy, wrinkled knees, and a big dappled-gray wooden horse with a black patent leather harness that Marcella had been given the Christmas before.

Each day when Marcella went off to school, and every night when she fell fast asleep, the dolls would tell each other stories and laugh and play together, just as your toys and dolls do when they are sure you aren't watching. And although Raggedy Ann and Andy loved all the other dolls, still at times they liked to leave Marcella's house together and walk down through the deep, deep woods that were filled with animals and birds and all sorts of surprising creatures, because there they found strange adventures.

So, this day, when the two Raggedys were sure that Marcella was on the school bus and her mother and father had already left for work, Raggedy Andy dragged a chair over to the window, and the two dolls climbed up and over the sill and tumbled to the ground outside. Since they were stuffed with cotton, it didn't hurt them a bit, and in a minute they were free and on their way.

2

The Raggedys had gone but a short distance, enjoying the crackle of autumn leaves beneath their feet, when Raggedy Ann heard something calling from the edge of the deep, deep woods.

"Didn't that sound like someone calling for help?" Raggedy Andy asked as he caught hold of Raggedy Ann's arm.

"I heard something, but I couldn't hear just what was said," Raggedy Ann replied in a whisper.

"Listen," Raggedy Andy said. "There it is again!"

"HELP! HELP!" someone cried.

"It's on the other side of that great big stone," Raggedy Ann said. "Let's go climb to the top of it so we can see who it is."

Up the stone they climbed by taking turns stepping on each

other's shoulders, until they could look down from the top. There was the Easter Bunny with his Easter basket—an unlikely creature indeed to come upon in October—and he kept on counting his eggs and crying, "Four! I've only got four eggs left!"

"But you have lots of time to paint more eggs before Easter," said Raggedy Ann, sliding down the other side of the rock. "This is the fall season—winter hasn't even come yet, and spring is many months away."

"That's the trouble," said the Easter Bunny. "My gardener has run off with my whole supply of spring bulbs. How will I know when it's spring next year if there are no snowdrops or crocuses to warn me; and if there are no yellow daffodils and red tulips, where will I get my pretty egg colors from?"

"Bulbs? What's a bulb?" asked Andy.

"Is it something you grow in a lamp?" asked Raggedy Ann.

"Oh, no," replied the Easter Bunny, peering sadly into his basket. "Spring bulbs are bulbs you plant in autumn, so that flowers will come up next spring."

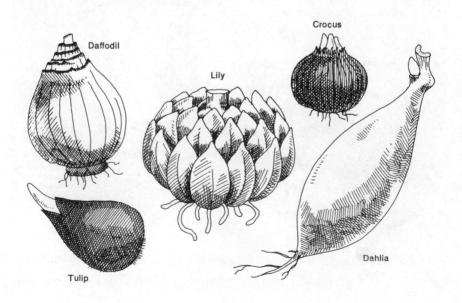

Daffodil

Crocus

Lily

Dahlia

Tulip

4

"But a bulb is made out of glass and lights up," said Andy, who thought the Easter Bunny wasn't making any sense.

"Not the kind of bulbs I'm talking about," snapped back the Easter Bunny. "A bulb is something like an onion, only in the center of it there is a tiny flower, with a tiny stem and leaves, and the outside layers of the bulb contain all the food the baby bud needs to grow. When you bury the bulb in the ground in September or October, or any time before the soil gets hard and cold, the bulb sends out roots in search of moisture and the bud starts to develop underneath the ground."

"You mean it's actually growing underground all winter while the rest of Nature is asleep?" asked Andy, thinking how cold the little buds must get under their blanket of earth and snow.

"Certainly," answered the Easter Bunny, nibbling a lettuce sandwich he had pulled out of his pocket, "and some of the smallest flowers have grown enough by the end of winter to poke their heads right out into the sunshine—even when there's still snow on the ground! That's how I can tell spring is really around the corner—spring bulbs are the first flowers to sprout and shout, 'SPRING IS HERE!' "

"We'd be glad to help you plant bulbs," said Raggedy Ann, "but first we'll have to find out where to get some and how to go about it."

"I know what we should do," exclaimed Raggedy Andy, running his fingers through his woolly hair. "Ask Mother Nature for some advice!"

And so the two Raggedys and the Easter Bunny set out in search of Mother Nature's house. They had not walked far down the path through the deep, deep woods before they came upon a tiny cottage at the edge of a stream, surrounded by flowers and all the creatures of the woods. Mother Nature had lived there when even the largest trees were only tiny little shoots, and every morning for thousands and thousands of years in the past (and for thousands of years to come!) she would scatter food upon the surface of the singing stream, and the lovely fish would leap from the water in a rainbow of splashing color.

Even the Mamma deers brought their wobbly-legged little fawns to meet Mother Nature. The clearing around her house was always full of butterflies and beautiful blossoms, and the air smelled sweet and clean.

"Come in, come in," said Mother Nature when she saw the three approaching. "You're the very people I was hoping to see. I've got some sacks of spring bulbs that must be planted before the frost is on the ground. Would you like to help?"

"We would!" cried the two Raggedys together. "And there are lots of girls and boys reading this book who would like to join in, too. Can you tell us what we need to know?"

"If I can't, I don't know who could," laughed Mother Nature, passing around mugs of steaming peppermint tea and a platter of hot biscuits and honey butter. "In fact, planting spring bulbs in autumn is as easy as it is fun, and I find that young people are especially good at it. Grown-ups like to plant them in rows which come up looking stiff and unnatural, but children like to scatter them about and bury them in bunches here and there, which is how I think spring bulbs look prettiest when they bloom."

"There are so many different kinds of bulbs in these sacks," said Raggedy Ann, sorting among them, "and some are much

too big to fit into my little apron pocket, but others are as small as baby radishes. Do you—"

"For Heaven's sake," interrupted the Easter Bunny impatiently, stuffing some of the larger ones into his basket, "the bigger ones are for the big three flowers of spring—daffodils, tulips and hyacinths. The little ones are the very earliest bulbs to bloom—snowdrops, winter aconite, crocuses, and glory-of-the-snow. There are also some little ones that bloom just a bit later, grape hyacinths and scilla. All of them will bloom faster if you plant them in a sunny spot instead of the shade, and each family of bulbs has so many different colors and varieties to choose from that it's almost like planting crayons—you can pick your own color combinations and arrange them any way you like.

"Of course, if you stand around blabbing all day, you'll never get any planting done at all," finished the Easter Bunny, scooping up a bunch of little bulbs in his hat and hopping out the door.

"Why is he so disagreeable?" asked Raggedy Andy. "Is it because his gardener stole his bulbs, and he's afraid there won't be any snowdrops or crocuses or daffodils next spring to let him know it's Easter time?"

"Nonsense!" laughed Mother Nature gently. "The Easter Bunny played a joke on you. You see, whenever a bulb is planted, it not only comes up the following spring, but also for many more springs to come, so there are always lots of crocuses peeking out each year to tell the Bunny to get busy, and lots of snowdrops to cheer us all up on a late winter day. The Easter Bunny loves all those spring bulbs so much that he tries to trick boys and girls, and anyone else who will lend a hand, into helping him plant new bulbs each autumn, so that each

8

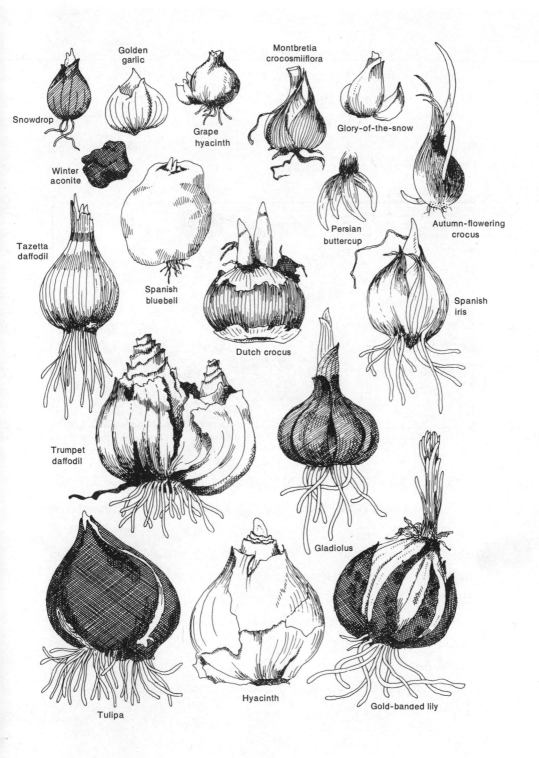

Snowdrop

Golden
garlic

Grape
hyacinth

Montbretia
crocosmiiflora

Glory-of-the-snow

Winter
aconite

Persian
buttercup

Autumn-flowering
crocus

Tazetta
daffodil

Spanish
bluebell

Dutch crocus

Spanish
iris

Trumpet
daffodil

Gladiolus

Tulipa

Hyacinth

Gold-banded lily

spring will be even more colorful than the one that went before!"

So the Raggedys gathered up some bulbs of each kind of flower and were on their way out of Mother Nature's house when Raggedy Ann suddenly thought of something. "Where will the boys and girls reading this book get bulbs to plant in their own yards in the fall?"

"Mister Muskrat is a good person to ask," answered Mother Nature. "You'll find him digging a hole in the bank of the Looking-glass Brook which runs by the back of my garden. And don't hesitate to come by again with any other questions you might have about growing things. That's what I like to talk about best!"

Soon they came upon a queer little dumpy creature standing in the water and digging a hole in the bank. He wore a little round felt hat, a purple bow tie and red suspenders, and you could tell by his eyeglasses that he was smart and knew a lot of things.

"Hello, Mister Muskrat," said Raggedy Andy. "We're off to plant some bulbs in the countryside, and we were hoping you could tell us where most people can get a good supply of bulbs each autumn, so they can plant some, too."

"When it's planting time, in September and October and November, you can get them in many neighborhood stores. In the grocery store, in the hardware store, and of course in all the stores where they sell flowers and plants. But there's another way boys and girls can choose from among the widest possible variety of bulbs—and have them sent right to their homes in the mail!"

"You mean the mailman can bring them right to Marcella's door? He must be Mother Nature's helper—and a great friend of the Easter Bunny too," laughed Raggedy Ann.

"Here's what you do," said Mister Muskrat. "You send a post card to one of the companies that sells seeds and bulbs and ask them to send you a catalog (that's a book showing pictures of the different kinds of flowers and vegetables that grow from the seeds and bulbs they sell). They'll send you a free catalog, and you can have a wonderful time picking out the plants you want to grow. Then you can order them directly through the mail. It's a good idea to write for the catalogs in the middle of summer—that way you can be sure there'll be plenty of time to order your bulbs for fall, but the companies will send you catalogs any time you write for them."

"Could you give us the names and addresses to write to?" asked Raggedy Andy. "I'm sure some of the boys and girls will want to send out their own post cards for catalogs—even if it's too late for some of them to order bulbs this fall."

"Got a pencil?" asked Mister Muskrat. "Here goes: **Park**

Seed Company, Greenwood, South Carolina 29646. And another: **Burpee Company, Philadelphia, Pennsylvania 19132** (there's also a **Burpee Company in Clinton, Iowa, 52732,** and in **Riverside, California 92502**—you should write to the one nearest you). The address of the **Harris Seed Company** is **64 Moreton Farm, Rochester, New York 14624. J. Howard French** sells all kinds of bulbs, and the address is **Baltimore Pike, Lima, Pennsylvania 19060,** and the most extraordinary bulb catalog I have ever seen comes from **P. deJager & Sons, 188 Ashbury Street, South Hamilton, Massachusetts 01982.** The catalogs are fun to receive in the mail and give you lots of good reading on a rainy day while you're trying to decide what to order."

"I'm going to order every one of them," said Raggedy Ann, who loved to get things in the mail. "One more thing—I guess we'll need a shovel if we're going to dig holes for bulbs. Can you tell us where we can get a shovel like yours?"

"Try Mr. Tubble's store. He has a grocery store, clothing store, toy store all rolled into one, and he has everything you'll need for planting bulbs, including lots of good gardening tips. Right now I'd better get back to my digging or I'll miss my dinner."

"What?" said Raggedy Andy, who couldn't quite figure out what digging had to do with dinner.

"I'LL MISS MY DINNER!" Mister Muskrat shouted, wondering how the Raggedys could hear anything at all, for he suddenly saw that neither of them had any ears. "SOMEONE HAS FILLED MY KITCHEN DOORWAY WITH MUD AND GRASS SO I CAN'T GET IN MY HOUSE."

"It sure is a good thing we don't have any ears," Raggedy

Ann giggled, "or you'd break our eardrums shouting like that."

"Who blocked your doorway up, Mister Muskrat?" asked Andy, who thought it would be terrible to be locked outside one's house at dinnertime.

"Timothy Turtle, that's who. I saw the footprints."

"How do you know it was Timothy?" Raggedy Ann wished to know.

"Because," said Mister Muskrat, "Timothy Turtle wears four shoes, two on his back feet and two on his front feet, and he turns them in pigeon-toed when he walks. So you see, he left four pigeon-toed tracks. Now I'm digging my kitchen doorway open again, for it's time I had my dinner!"

Just then Timothy Turtle came walking pigeon-toed around the bend in the bank and tipped his hat to Raggedy Ann, although to do this he had to take off one of his front shoes.

"Well, here you are hard at work, Mister Muskrat! Building a new house, I suppose?"

Mister Muskrat winked at the Raggedys and said, "Sit down here beside our two friends, Timothy Turtle, and I will soon be through!" And with this Mister Muskrat made the dirt fly un-

13

til he had opened his doorway—and buried the shoe Timothy
Turtle had taken off. Then he went inside and came out with
two large slices of Muskrat bread and butter and jam and gave

one to Timothy Turtle. "I know that you Raggedys do not eat,"
he laughed, "because your mouths are only painted on."

The Raggedys smiled at each other, but didn't say a word.
As soon as Timothy Turtle finished eating, he looked around

for his missing front shoe. "Can't seem to find it; guess I'll have to stop by Mr. Tubble's store for a new shoe," he yawned. Turtles are always sleepy because they have to carry their heavy houses on their backs.

"That's where we're headed, too," said Raggedy Andy. "Perhaps you can show us the way."

And off they went, Timothy Turtle leading the way with only three shoes, Raggedy Andy second in line with a sack of spring bulbs, and Raggedy Ann last of all because she was slowed down not only by the bulbs she was carrying, but also by the shoe she had secretly rescued from the mud. You see, Raggedy Ann is always very kind—she has a candy heart sewn into her chest, and the letters on it spell out, "I LOVE YOU."

CHAPTER TWO

TULIP-O-MANIA!

O N THEIR WAY to Mr. Tubble's store they came to Granny Field-mouse's house, which was the cutest, smallest house the Raggedys had ever seen. Granny Field-mouse, who was only two inches tall, wore a tiny lace cap, a flowered dress and a little white apron, and she was sweeping her front porch when she saw the Raggedys walking by.

"Won't you rest for a while?" asked Granny Field-mouse. "Where are you going in such a hurry, and what are you carrying in those sacks?"

"Spring bulbs," said Raggedy Andy. "We must get them into the ground fast if they are going to be ready to come up by spring."

"Bulbs!" exclaimed Granny, with a twinkle in here eye. "I

know all about bulbs—let me take off my apron and walk along with you."

So the four of them set out for Mr. Tubble's store, which they came upon at the next bend of the deep, deep woods.

"We need a shovel so we can plant our spring bulbs, Mr. Tubble," said Raggedy Ann when they entered the store. "And we need some advice! We never have planted anything before. I hope it won't be hard."

"Bulbs are so easy even Timothy Turtle here could do it, and you know he has a hard time just keeping track of his shoes!" laughed Mr. Tubble. "Bulbs don't need weeding, they don't really need feeding the first year you plant them, they don't need to be watered, they don't need to be watched!"

"You mean you just dig a hole and drop in a bulb?" asked Raggedy Andy.

"It's not much harder than that," answered Mr. Tubble. "In fact, bulbs are so little work that the real fun of planting them comes from picking out the different kinds of flowers you want to plant, selecting different shapes and colors, figuring out where they should go in the yard, and which should be next to which. You can look through a bulb catalog, or a picture book about bulbs, and see how the different varieties look when they are in bloom. It's just like creating a painting: you put some blue grape hyacinths here in this corner next to some white tulips, or maybe some red hyacinths in that corner next to some yellow daffodils."

"We've already got our bulbs for this year," said Raggedy Ann, "but next year we will get plenty of daydreaming in before we buy our bulbs, and we *would* like to know more about the different kinds."

"Right now we need a shovel so we can get started," said Raggedy Andy. "Have you got the kind we need?"

"Let's see," said Mr. Tubble, looking around the store, "you will need a big shovel, which we call a *spade,* and a little shovel that fits in your hand, which we call a *trowel.* And if you are going to be doing any more gardening at all during the year, you really should have a small number of tools to help you with different kinds of planting chores.

"In addition to a spade for digging big holes and a trowel for digging small ones, you will need a *rake* to help crumble the soil, to smooth it out and help get the pebbles and large twigs away from the area you are working on. You might also want a *hoe,* which chops up the clumps of earth you dig out with your spade into smaller pieces, and a small *hand cultivator,* which looks like a claw and helps break up and loosen the soil close to your plants so they can get plenty of air and light. I have tools in several different sizes, so you probably ought to pick the smallest ones with the shortest handles. They'll be easier for you to use than the biggest ones I have."

"Do we need all those tools for planting bulbs," asked Raggedy Ann, "or can we buy only the ones we need and get the others next spring?"

"Suit yourself," said Mr. Tubble. "But it's a good idea to get the basic tools you will need for various kinds of gardening, and paint the handles with a bright color and put your names on them. That way you can find them easily when they are lying in the grass as you plant your flowers. There's one rule you should always remember: never *ever* leave the sharp sides of your tools facing up! Someone might step on them and lose a foot! And always clean off your tools when you are finished

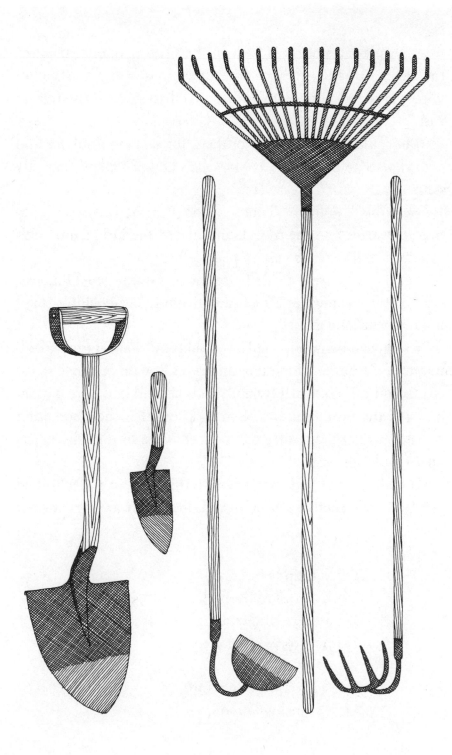

using them, and put them back in the shed or the basement or the closet in which they belong. Once in a while you should wipe the metal parts with grease or oil to keep them free of rust."

"But could you keep some of them for us now until we find a good place to keep them at Marcella's house?" asked Raggedy Ann.

"Certainly," said Mr. Tubble. "For planting bulbs you only need the spade and the trowel, and maybe the little hand culti-vator too. Bulbs are so easy to plant—"

"And such a treat to eat!" squealed Granny Field-mouse, who had been quiet as a mouse until now, but couldn't stand it a moment longer.

"I forgot to mention," said Mr. Tubble, "that Granny Field-mouse and Charlie Chipmunk and even Ronald Rat love to eat crocus and tulip bulbs! Hyacinth and daffodil bulbs are poison-ous, and the little creatures seem to know that these shouldn't be eaten, even though they feel perfectly free to turn the others into a midnight snack."

"It makes my mouth water just to think about it," admitted Granny Field-mouse. "Would you like to hear my favorite song?

> Oh, a tulip bulb,
> With a crust of fresh dirt,
> Is a lovely Sunday dinner,
> With a crocus for dessert.

> But I never eat a hyacinth,
> Or a crunchy daffodil,

For I know whoever eats those bulbs,
Grows feverish and ill.

Yes, I love a juicy tulip,
And a crocus bulb or two,
And I often dig up five or six
For a hearty autumn stew.

I know I shouldn't do it,
I know I should desist,
But a tulip bulb for dinner
Is too tasty to resist!

"When Freda and Freddie Field-mouse were little mice, I used to squeak them to sleep with that lullaby," sighed Granny Field-mouse.

"How does Granny get at the bulbs if they're buried in the ground?" asked Raggedy Andy, beginning to see why Granny Field-mouse had been so eager to come along.

"She uses the tunnels dug by Martin and Marietta Mole," explained Mr. Tubble. "If some of the tulips you plant this fall don't come up next spring, you'll know who's to blame—don't blame the moles!"

"What can we do then?" asked Raggedy Ann.

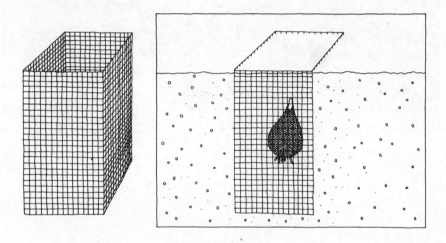

"You can make a little wire cage for each tulip bulb before you plant it, using wire mesh (with ¼-inch spaces) from the hardware store, or you can try dusting each bulb with a chemical called rotenone. Another trick that often works is mothballs. You plunk a few in the hole you dig, right next to each bulb.

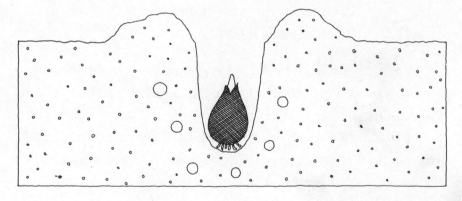

Sometimes a cat keeps the mice away from your garden, but if it turns out that you really have a great number of Granny Field-mouse's friends around your house, it's better to plant extra daffodils and leave the tulips for someone else's yard."

"Looks like we're ready," said the two Raggedys, hoisting up their shovels and their packages of bulbs.

"Mind if I come along?" asked Mr. Tubble. "I can tell you how deep to dig, and give some other hints along the way."

So off they marched: Timothy Turtle with his fourth shoe back on again; the two Raggedys with all their equipment; Granny Field-mouse, hoping some spare tulip bulbs would accidently roll her way; and Mr. Tubble with some little sticks and labels so they could mark the spots in the ground where the different batches of bulbs were planted.

"Bulbs look best planted in groups with other bulbs of the same kind and color," said Mr. Tubble. "Let's plant the little bulbs that come up earliest on the sunny side of Marcella's house, where you can see them through the window when they come into bloom at the end of winter—when it's still too cold to stay outdoors for long. It's always a good idea to plant bulbs, big or small, around things in the yard—around a rock, or next to the garden gate, or along the path leading to the house, or in front of an evergreen bush.

"You can plant little blue or white glory-of-the-snow along the side of a cellar wall. I bet that would be a lovely surprise for Marcella! Snowdrops, which are little white flowers shaped like a bell and tipped with green, love moisture, so you can plant a bunch near her outdoor faucet, or not too far from her rain spout. Winter aconite, which look like yellow buttercups with

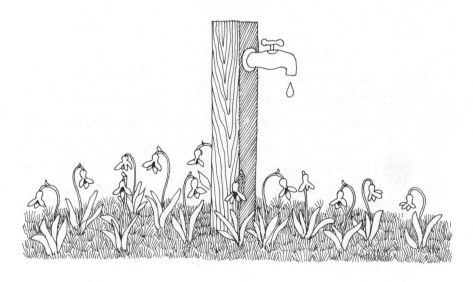

a ruffled green collar, can nestle around the milk box, and you can plant little circles of grape hyacinths around the clothesline pole in back. They're called grape hyacinths, although their real name is *Muscari,* because they look like tiny deep-blue grape clusters on a green stem, but they also come in white.

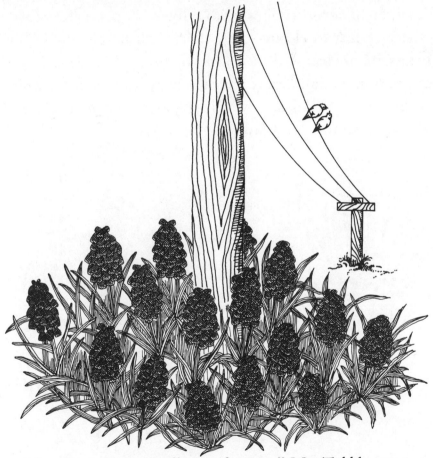

"Crocuses are practically my favorite," Mr. Tubble went on, casting a stern glance at Granny Field-mouse as the Raggedys and their friends walked toward Marcella's house. "You can plant them on either side of the front door, facing the sun, and if the boys and girls reading this want to be sure they get the kind of crocuses that bloom by the end of winter, they should buy the ones labeled 'Species Crocus' or 'Snow Crocus' or 'Winter-Flowering Crocus'—these are smaller and come up faster than the larger 'Dutch Crocus.' In fact, the Snow Crocuses that bloom early and are especially pretty belong to the following families: *Susianus* (yellow with brown stripes); *Korolkowi* (the very first to bloom—deep violet with purple and yellow stripes, bronze base); the *Chrysanthus* group (a wide variety of colors, from Cream Beauty which is ivory, to Blue Pearl which is silver blue, to Advance which is yellow and bronze); and *Tomasiniaus* (beautiful lavender blooms).

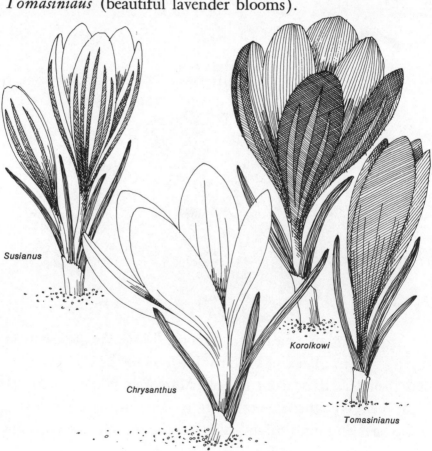

Susianus

Korolkowi

Chrysanthus

Tomasinianus

"Dutch crocuses come up a little later and are bigger than the Species. Popular varieties include Yellow Mammoth, which are golden yellow, and Pickwick, which are powder blue with purple stripes. You can be a crocus artist—just decide which colors you like the best, and Mother Nature will do the rest!" laughed Mr. Tubble.

"Now I have to admit that daffodils are my very favorite bulbs—and each year more daffodils come up than the year before! There are many varieties, and all of them look lovely in 'drifts' scattered near a tree, or along a path or a row of hedges. The names of some that never fail to surprise and delight all the woodland creatures are King Alfred (big and yellow, as is Golden Harvest and Unsurpassable); Beersheba (big, white, and very early to flower); Mary Copeland (a spectacular double daffodil that is white, yellow and orange!); Poeticus (white petals and a dark red eye); and Trevithian (two or three small lemon yellow flowers to each stem).

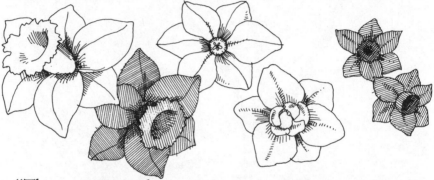

"There are some other very tiny ones which are as charming as they are hard to find—W. P. Milner, Angel's Tears, and Hoop Petticoat. Two or three next to a small rock look like a garden made by elves!"

"Just the thing for Ned Gnome's garden," observed Timothy Turtle, who wanted it understood that he was taking all this in.

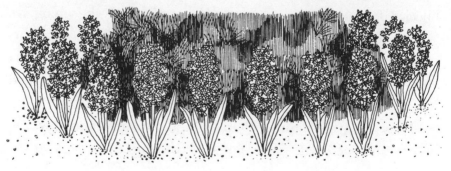

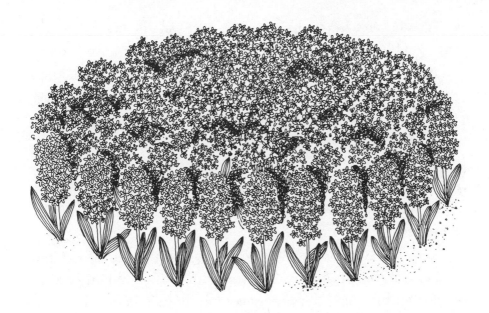

"As for hyacinths, which stand as stiff and straight as little soldiers, they come in white, pink, blue, yellow and red," continued Mr. Tubble. "They look nice as a border for a path, or marching single file in a ring around a bush, or you can plant two or three of one color together in a little patch. It's better not to get the biggest size bulbs, because they turn into flowers that are so big and heavy they can hardly hold their heads up by themselves! Some nice ones to look for are Bismarck (blue), Delft's Blue (bright blue), Ostara and Marie (dark blue), and Perle Brillante (sky blue); Pink Pearl (rosy), Eros (deep pink), and Anna Marie (clear pink); Edelweiss and L'Innocence (white); Jan Bos (red, and early to flower); and Amethyst (violet)."

"I can't imagine how anyone ever decides which ones to plant," groaned Raggedy Andy. "Each one sounds so beautiful, it would take me weeks to make up my mind!"

"You haven't heard the worst of it yet—or the best," laughed Mr. Tubble. "For when it comes to tulips, there have been so many kinds developed in different people's gardens that tulip gardeners were once called Tulip-o-maniacs!

"The short-stemmed ones, which bloom early in spring, are called Species tulips," explained Mr. Tubble. "Species tulips, like Species crocuses, are the kinds that Mother Nature originally grew herself, and that is why they often are smaller than the kinds later developed by Tulip-o-maniacs, who naturally thought that 'big' means 'better.'

"*Clusiana* is an unusually nice one in this group. It is red and white, and some people call it Peppermint Stick. Another kind of Species tulips are the *Fosteriana* family members, which not only bloom early, but actually have huge, bright flowers. There are three kinds of *Fosteriana* I am sure you would enjoy: Red Emperor, which is a beautiful red; Purissima, the only white one; and a yellow one called Egg Beater.

"*Kaufmanniana* are the earliest kind of the Species tulips to bloom, and they are shaped like water lilies! If you come across any *Kaufmanniana* varieties, you should be sure to get some, because folks will come from miles around just to see them.

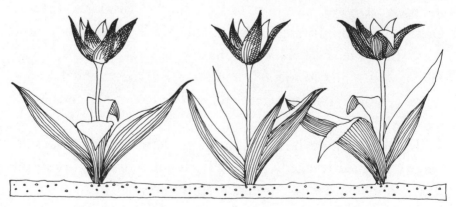

Scarlet Elegance is a *Kaufmanniana* that is fiery red with a yellow center, and it is so pretty it makes your eyes pop out!"

"I'll tell you what's popping out—my brain!" said Timothy Turtle. "How can anyone remember all these fancy names?"

"You don't have to remember them," said Raggedy Ann, "but it is fun to know something about all the different kinds. That way, when you get your catalog or go into a plant store, you'll have some idea about what all the different names mean."

"Okay," grumbled Timothy. "But I hope there isn't too much more—a turtle's brain is a delicate thing and must be treated gently."

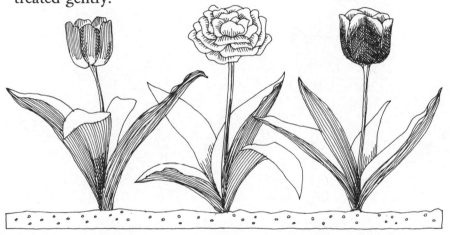

"Now we come to the tulips that most people think of when they talk about tulips. The first of these are called Single Early tulips, and some nice ones to look for are Bellona (golden yellow), Christmas Marvel (cherry pink), Charles (deep red with a yellow base), and Ralph (lemon yellow). Blooming around the same time as these are the Double Early tulips (double means they have many more petals and look almost like peonies!), and if you want to try a few of these, get Peach Blossom —peachy pink.

"The next ones to bloom are Mendel tulips and Triumph tulips. Of the Mendel tulips, Bing Crosby is deep red, and Her Grace is white with a border of rose. A lovely Triumph variety is called Elmus, which is red edged with white.

"Then come the Darwin hybrids, with tall stems and huge flowers. Here you should look for Oxford, which is pure red, and an orange-red one called Apeldoorn. After these come the Lily-Flowered tulips, which look like lilies! Two Lily-Flowered tulips you will like are Queen of Sheba, which is brownish-red and orange, and White Triumphator, which is—"

"White!" said Timothy.

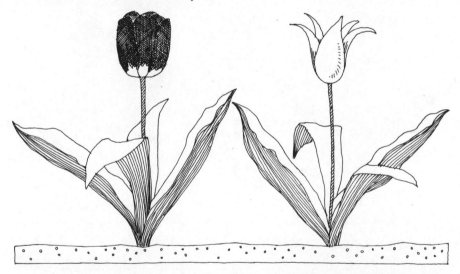

"Right!" said Mr. Tubble. "Later in May come the famous Darwin tulips (they are even taller than the Darwin hybrids we just mentioned), and my favorite is the Darwin tulip called Clara Butt, which is a shimmery orange-pink, and it goes on blooming spring after spring after spring without ever getting tired out! Sunkist is also nice—it's a deep yellow, and the Darwin called Insurpassable is violet."

34

"A group of yellow Sunkists next to a group of violet Insurpassables would certainly be a beautiful sight!" said Raggedy Andy, whose favorite colors were yellow and purple.

"Finally come the startling Parrot tulips, which are *fringed* all around their petals! Karel Doorman is the name of a Parrot tulip that is red with a fringed border of yellow, and they are practically the prettiest tulip I know."

"But how could anyone ever plant that many different kinds of tulip bulbs?" gasped Raggedy Andy. "My head is swimming just from hearing about them all!"

"Of course," chuckled Mr. Tubble, "no one could possibly have the time or the money to plant all those kinds of tulips! And I haven't even mentioned all of them! But each year you might want to experiment with a few bulbs that you didn't plant the year before, to see which ones you like the best. After all, the old ones from past years will be coming up again next spring anyway, so you can compare them with the new ones you plant when they're all in bloom. You should keep a record of which ones are planted where, so you'll know their names when they come into bloom.

"Also, if you keep the different flowering times for the different kinds of tulips in mind, you can plant some that bloom early *(Kaufmanniana, Fosteriana),* some that come up in the middle of spring (Single Early, Double Early, Mendel, Triumph), and some that come at the end of spring (Darwin, Parrot). And it's nice to plant the tall tulips in a row along a fence, while planting clumps of short ones near a path or a front step."

"You could make a little tulip garden," suggested Granny Field-mouse. "In the back row you plant a few tall Darwins, in the next row some Parrots (because they are shorter than the Darwins), then a row of Lily-Flowered tulips (because they're shorter than the Parrots), then a row of Triumphs or Mendels which are shorter still; in front of these you put a small row of Single Early tulips (shorter than Triumphs or Mendels), and in the very front row you plant some *Fosteriana,* if you want a front row with fat blossoms, or you could make the front row out of the very short water-lily–shaped *Kaufmanniana* tulips that bloom earliest of all.

"That way," she continued, licking her lips, "you can watch them bloom one row at a time. Starting from the front row, which is the earliest and has the shortest stemmed tulips, each row that follows will be a bit taller and later to bloom than the one right in front of it."

"Maybe we'll do that next year," said Raggedy Ann, "when we have more time to gather up some of each kind. This year we'd better worry about getting the ones we have put into the ground."

"Mr. Tubble," said Raggedy Andy, "could you show us how to plant our bulbs? I hope it isn't as complicated as it was to learn about their names," he laughed.

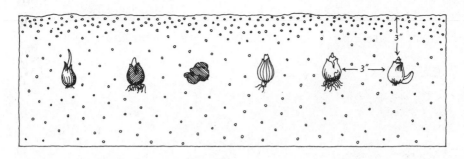

"It's simple," replied Mr. Tubble. "The little bulbs—crocus, scilla, winter aconite, snowdrops, grape hyacinths and glory-of-the-snow—go into the soil about 3 inches deep and 3 inches apart. The big bulbs—daffodils, tulips and hyacinths—go in about 6 inches deep and 6 inches apart, except for the very small varieties of tulips and daffodils which only need to be planted about 5 inches deep and 5 inches apart.

"There are two ways to put them into the ground, and both of them are easy. The easier way is this: you take your spade

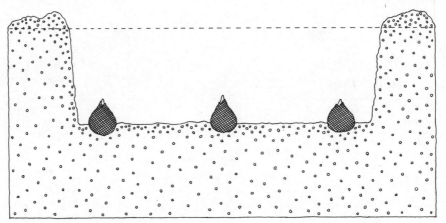

and dig up a small area in which you'd like to plant a group of bulbs of one kind, and with a ruler you measure whether it's deep enough for the kind you want to plant there. Then you pour some water onto the bottom of it and let it drain, arrange your bulbs *pointed end up* on the soil the correct distance apart from each other, and cover them up with the soil you just dug up!"

"Is that all?" asked Raggedy Ann.

"Just about," said Mr. Tubble. "The other way you can do it, if you want to plant one at a time (for example, if you have a spot big enough for only one crocus), is to make a small hole

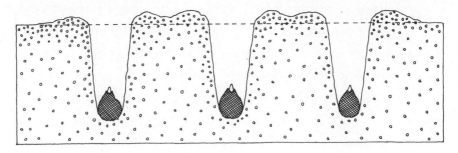

with your trowel and drop the bulb in. Push the earth back in the hole, and it's done!"

"Isn't there *anything* else we should know?" asked Raggedy Andy.

"Well," said Mr. Tubble, "don't pick a spot where there is usually a puddle of water after it rains, because bulbs don't like to have their feet stay wet! *And don't plant any bulbs where the lawn is usually mowed* in the spring—the green leaves and stems of *all* bulb plants have to remain in the sun, *after* the flower has finished blooming, until they turn yellow. That is because the leaves are actually using the sunshine to make a *new* supply of food to store in the bulb beneath the ground— food that will nourish next year's flower as it begins to form inside the bulb.

"This is very important to remember. If you pick off the leaves in spring or mow them off accidentally with the lawn mower before they have made up a new batch of bulb food, no new flower will come up the next spring, because the baby bud will have been starved!

"Two other things are also important to keep in mind each spring: as soon as the flower has finished blooming, pick off the dead blossom with your fingers, along with the little round seed pod that you will notice at the top of the stem right below the flower. Otherwise, the developing seeds will eat up all the food and none will be sent down to renew the bulb.

"The other thing is bonemeal. When the leaves are making up the food in spring for next year's flower, they need an ingredient called *phosphorous* as part of their recipe. Bonemeal contains phosphorous, and you can get it in a little bag at plant and hardware stores. If you mix some bonemeal into the soil on

the bottom of the hole when you first plant the bulbs in the fall, it will be waiting there when the plant needs it the next spring."

"Should we plant some kinds of bulbs before others?" asked Timothy Turtle, who was getting very impatient, but he thought it would be a smart question to ask.

"Most people plant bulbs in September and October, but tulips are better off if you wait a bit and plant them close to November," said Mr. Tubble.

"Mercy!" exclaimed Raggedy Ann. "We'd better get busy digging! There are so many spots I'd like to plant bulbs in— why I bet we could even plant some little bulbs between the rocks on the hill where Bertram Bear lives," she added, remembering how sad Bertram had been last spring when flowers were blooming in everyone's yard but his. "I'm going to call all the woodland creatures together to help with the fall planting, so that next spring will be the prettiest one we've ever had!"

So all the creatures came from far and near. Mister and Missus Muskrat came, and Ms. Henrietta Hedgehog came, and Easter and Esther Bunny came with their baby, Bettina Bunny,

Martin Mole arrived and brought his whole family (since they could dig holes faster and deeper than anyone else!), and even Granny Field-mouse's grandchildren were invited after they promised not to eat the crocus and tulip bulbs.

They dug and planted, dug and planted, until every last bulb of every kind they had was tucked snugly into the ground.

When they were finished, they celebrated their efforts with a great big party. Raggedy Ann used the magic wishing pebble that was sewn inside her body and wished for ice cream sodas for all her guests and woodland friends.

And you know what? Some people say that if you have an ice cream soda after you finish planting your bulbs, the flowers will be especially beautiful when they come up next spring. Now that's another important thing to keep in mind!

CHAPTER THREE

READY, SET—BLOOM!

RAGGEDY ANN and Andy were in the middle of enjoy-ing the ice cream sodas with all the other woodland creatures who had helped with the bulb planting, when all of a sudden Raggedy Ann exclaimed, "Goodness! How dark it is getting—we had better run back to Marcella's house and climb in the window before it gets any later." So they waved goodbye to their friends and set off for home, taking along some extra spring bulbs in their pockets as souvenirs of their adventure.

When they arrived at the house they climbed over the sill and arranged themselves as Marcella had left them—that way she might not notice they'd been out all day. Raggedy Andy got into bed and pulled the blanket over his head, but poor

Raggedy Ann had to get back into the strangest position on the floor where Marcella had dropped her that morning—sprawled with her arms and legs sticking out in all directions. Her yarn hair lay twisted over one side of her face, hiding one of her shoe-button eyes.

"Did you ever see such an odd-looking creature?" said a voice Raggedy Ann didn't recognize.

"It has shoe-buttons for eyes!" said another voice. "And yarn hair!"

"Did you ever see such horrible feet!" continued the first voice. "With garden dirt all over its shoes!"

Henny, the Dutch doll, rolled off the top of the toy chest and said "Mamma" in his quavery voice, he was so surprised to hear anyone insulting Raggedy Ann—sweet Raggedy with her candy heart, whom all the dolls loved.

Uncle Clem, the Scottish doll, was also surprised—and angry. He walked up to the two new dolls who had been talking so meanly about Raggedy Ann and looked them straight in the eyes. "I'd like to bop you right on your heads with Marcella's broom handle," he said, "but you've got so much hair you probably wouldn't feel a thing." Uncle Clem couldn't help being a bit jealous, since lately a lot of his yarn hair had been falling out from underneath his red hat.

The two new dolls had come in the mail that morning. Marcella had named them Annabel-Lee and Thomas, after her aunt and uncle who had sent them, and they were not only beautifully dressed in old-fashioned costumes, but had *real* hair with masses of shiny curls.

When Uncle Clem walked in front of them and wagged his finger scoldingly, they laughed out loud. "Tee-hee-hee," they snickered. "He has holes in his knees!"

Uncle Clem shook, but he felt so hurt he thought he was going to cry. He walked over and sat down beside Raggedy Ann and brushed her yarn hair out of her shoe-button eye. "Don't you mind what they say, Raggedy," he said. "They don't know you like the rest of us do."

Pretty soon Annabel-Lee and Thomas stopped whispering, and their eyelids began to close. They were very tired from being in the mail all week and hadn't gotten any sleep. All of a sudden there was a loud noise as Annabel-Lee fell off her chair and Thomas slid to the floor, but the two of them were so sound asleep they went right on snoozing where they lay.

The two Raggedys got up and tiptoed over to them gently and lifted the two new dolls onto Raggedy Ann and Andy's bed. Raggedy Ann tucked them in snugly and lay down next to Andy on the hard floor.

The tin soldier and Uncle Clem both tried to coax the Raggedys into accepting their bed (they slept together in a wooden crate), but the Raggedys wouldn't hear of it. "We are stuffed with nice soft cotton, so the floor doesn't bother us a bit."

At daybreak the next morning, Annabel-Lee and Thomas woke to find themselves in the Raggedy's bed, and as they raised their heads to look at each other they felt terribly ashamed about the way they'd acted the night before. "How good and kind she looks," said Annabel-Lee when she saw Raggedy Ann asleep in a corner of the floor. "It must be her shoe-button eyes!"

"How nicely her wool hair falls in loops over her face," exclaimed Thomas. "I didn't notice how pleasant her face looked last night. We were wrong to laugh at her clothes, and I wish we could do something special to make up for how badly we behaved."

"I heard Raggedy Ann say something about planting bulbs outdoors—maybe we should show her how beautiful bulbs can look when they are planted *indoors*," Annabel-Lee said. She and Thomas had learned all about indoor gardens and plants when they had lived with Marcella's aunt and uncle in the city.

"What a good idea!" exclaimed Thomas. "Raggedy Ann, wake up! We've something to show you!"

Soon all the dolls were awake and eager to learn the secrets of growing spring bulbs indoors, where they could enjoy them right in their very own room. Raggedy Ann had brought some extra bulbs home with her the night before, but she had never expected to plant them inside the house!

"There are many spring bulbs, big and small, that you can play a little trick on," said Annabel-Lee. "You plant them in a container—a flower pot, a pretty bowl, a tin can, a jar, or even one of Henny's wooden shoes!—and then you put them in a cool, dark place, like the cellar or the garage or a closet that isn't near a heater or a hot water pipe, and let them grow their

roots just as they do beneath the ground outside. It's a good idea to cover the containers with a box to keep it dark while the bulbs are rooting, and it's necessary to keep the soil around the bulbs moist—like the snow and rain do outdoors in winter time.

"After eight to twelve weeks have passed (closer to eight weeks for the little bulbs you plant, and closer to twelve weeks for the biggest tulips), you can move the pots out of their cold

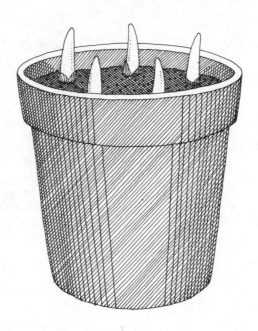

hiding place. You will see the green shoots growing out of the top soil in the containers, and they should be about 2 inches tall before you take them out from cold storage—daffodils should be even taller, about 3 inches, and tulips should stay in hiding until they are close to 6 inches high!

"Then you bring them into a regular part of the house that is cool and shady, and you watch them grow their stems and leaves taller and longer, and you can see them developing their buds. You must remember to keep them watered, though, or they will wither and get sick," said Annabel-Lee.

"When two weeks or so have passed, and you think they look strong and ready to bloom, move them into a sunny spot, and —presto! All that warm sun and bright light will make them think, SPRING IS HERE! and they will begin to bloom before your eyes in a few days!" continued Thomas, picking up where Annabel-Lee had left off.

"It's called 'forcing' bulbs," Thomas explained, "because you force them to flower earlier than they would if they'd been planted outdoors. I mean, you sort of make them believe it's spring, when it isn't really spring yet, by making it 'feel' like springtime indoors!"

"I have something else to add," said Annabel-Lee, tossing her pretty curls around and skipping over to Marcella's window. "If you give them *too much* direct sunlight, the heat will force them to bloom *too quickly* and to die too quickly. But if you find a spot that's just right, sunny but not too sunny and hot, your blooms may last several weeks or more!"

"And you don't have to force all your plants at once," said Thomas. "You can bring some bulbs out of hiding first, and leave others in storage until later—that way, you can have some new ones to force after the first ones have finished blooming."

"What wonderful secrets to know!" laughed Raggedy Ann, clapping her hands delightedly, for she loved the idea of flowers growing in Marcella's room in winter.

"What kinds of bulbs are best to force?" asked Andy, hoping the extra bulbs they had left over from planting outside would turn out to be right for forcing indoors.

"The same ones you planted outdoors," said Thomas, "except for the delicate little Species tulips and Species crocuses, which don't always work out so well and look kind of feeble when they are forced."

"How do we plant them?" asked Raggedy Ann.

"You get some potting soil from the plant store or the grocery store or the 5&10. You also get a small bag of coarse sand from the hardware store, or from a store where they sell builders' supplies, so that you can mix some in with the potting soil to keep the soil loose and crumbly. You don't *have* to do this, of course, but potting soil by itself tends to get packed down hard after a while, and bulbs don't grow as well as they do when the soil is light and sandy."

"Could we use sand from the beach?" asked Raggedy Ann.

"Certainly, if the sand has lots of tiny pebbles in it and isn't too fine. But if the sand comes from a saltwater beach, you must wash away the salt before you mix it into the potting soil, by giving it a bath in a bucket under an outdoor water faucet," he answered.

"Then you line up your containers and make sure each one has a drainage hole in the bottom to let extra water run out, and you place some pebbles (or pieces of broken flower pots)

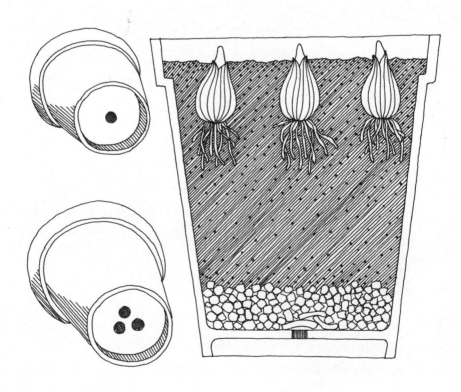

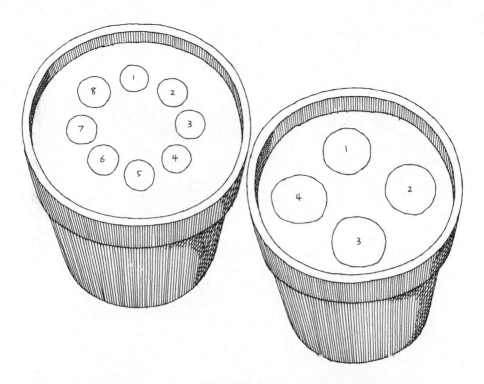

over the hole so that when you fill the container, the soil won't get jammed into the hole and block it up," continued Thomas.

"Next, you take one of the pots and fill it at least half full of earth. You shouldn't plant different kinds of bulbs in one container, so you decide which kind of bulbs go into which container, and then you make a label and put it on the front of it. For instance, it might say: KING ALFRED DAFFODILS.

"Now you place the bulbs on the soil, pointed end facing up, so that the tips of the bulbs are about level with the top edge of the container. You may have to add or remove some soil to get the bulbs to the right height. Little bulbs can be almost touching each other—you can plant six or eight of them in a pot, side by side—but big bulbs should have about an inch between them in the pot."

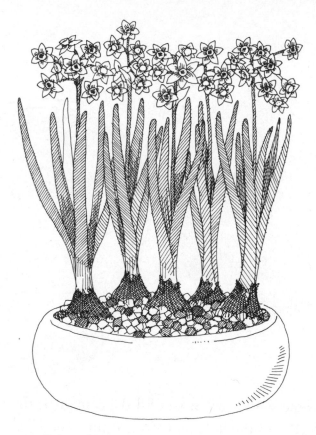

It's my turn," laughed Annabel-Lee. "Next, you fill in some soil between the bulbs in the container, *but you leave the tips showing above the soil.* Then you give them a good drink of water and put them away in whatever cold, dark place you have chosen. But you must remember to peek at them every few days to make sure the soil is moist and add a little water if it feels dry."

"There are some kinds of bulbs that don't even have to be grown in soil!" said Thomas. "Hyacinths and certain kinds of daffodils can be grown in water, and they are perfect for forcing early indoors. These special kinds of daffodils are called Paperwhite narcissus, Chinese Sacred Lily, and Soleil d'Or (that's French for Golden Sun), and they grow so fast they will flower on your window sill in three to five weeks! They don't need any time in cold storage at all (they've already had their cold storage before you buy them)."

"Three to five weeks!" exclaimed Raggedy Ann. "That means we could have them in bloom for Thanksgiving if we plant them now, and the ones we plant in November will be ready for Christmas!"

"But how do you plant them if they don't need soil?" asked Raggedy Andy.

"Easy," said Annabel-Lee. "You put some pebbles in a tray or a shallow container, add enough water so that it stays below the top pebbles, and set the bulbs right on top (remember, bulbs don't like their feet to stay wet). That way you can watch the roots forming as well as the stems and leaves!"

"And you can have all kinds of fun growing hyacinths in water too," said Thomas. "You can place a hyacinth bulb in the

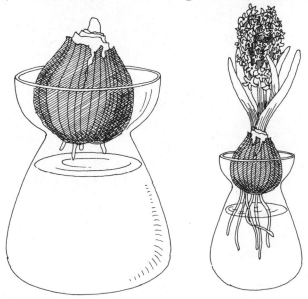

top of a small jar so it only fits halfway through the opening, and fill the bottom with water that doesn't quite touch the base of the bulb. The roots will grow down into the jar to reach the water, and the bulb will stay nice and dry.

"*Roman* hyacinths, like the Paperwhite narcissus, have been pre-cooled before you buy them, and they don't need cold storage at all. But they do need darkness, or they will begin to bloom before their flower spikes are tall enough, so you should tuck them away in the cabinet beneath the kitchen sink, or in a closet, or you might even make them a hat by turning an empty flower pot upside down on top of their container until you think the spikes are big enough to greet the light of day!" finished Thomas.

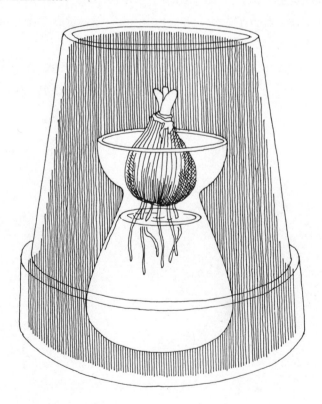

"You can grow regular hyacinths the same way, but they will need their period of cold storage," Annabel-Lee reminded the dolls. "Some people put them in the bottom of their refrigerators, so they can check the water level and have the fun of seeing the roots and spikes emerge."

"Oh, it will be so beautiful in Marcella's room this winter, I can hardly wait to get started," said Raggedy Ann. "We could decorate the containers in all sorts of pretty ways. We could

wrap the flower pots in tin foil, with a big tin foil collar and a ribbon, or we could paint designs on them with enamel paint and varnish them to keep them waterproof and clean. I am going to give a pitcher of Paperwhites to the Easter Bunny for Thanksgiving, and a dish of crocuses to Mother Nature for Christmas!"

"Have you any other indoor gardening tricks?" asked Raggedy Andy. But before Annabel-Lee could answer, they heard Marcella coming down the hall.

They all scurried to their resting places just in time to be silent and still as Marcella walked into the room.

"What's going on here!" said Marcella to the dolls, although she didn't expect any answer, of course, and the dolls said not one word. "Raggedy, you are full of dirt—why you look like you've been playing outdoors!" Marcella scolded, picking Raggedy Ann up from the floor. "You'd better have a bath and a shampoo, and put on some clean clothes. And that goes for you too, Raggedy Andy."

And so the two Raggedys gave a big smile to Annabel-Lee and Thomas, and went off with Marcella for a good scrubbing, glad that *all* the dolls had become the very best of friends.

CHAPTER FOUR

MOTHER EARTH

MOTHER NATURE was telling a good morning story to Bettina Bunny when she thought she heard footsteps —someone was running along the woodland path. She looked up just in time to see the two Raggedys skipping into the clearing, and she could tell they were full of excitement.

"Guess what we have done this morning!" said Raggedy Ann, breathlessly. "If you can solve this riddle, you'll know what it is:

> What goes in a pot
> But has to stay cold?
> What kind of grown-up
> Is five weeks old?

What grows in water
But never gets wet?
What fills up a dish
But never gets et?

What says, "Wake up! Spring is here!"
When it isn't yet that time of year?

"Let's see," said Mother Nature. "What goes in a pot but has to stay cold? A tulip bulb, or maybe a daffodil bulb, which you put in a container for forcing indoors. What kind of grown-up is five weeks old? My Paperwhite narcissus—it's sometimes big enough and ready to bloom even in three weeks! What grows in water but never gets wet? A hyacinth bulb. What fills up a dish but never gets et? A dish of crocuses! What says, 'Wake up! Spring is here!' when it isn't yet that time of year? All my spring bulbs, when they're forced early indoors! Am I right?"

"You are. Now can you guess what we've done?"

"You've planted bulbs for forcing in Marcella's room, and now you can hardly wait 'til they bloom! Goodness," exclaimed Mother Nature, with a laugh, "I've caught your rhyming habit, Raggedys."

"Look—here comes Johnny Cricket and his family," said Raggedy Andy, pointing down the path.

"I guess they are getting ready to move into their winter home. They do that every autumn when the first frost coats the leaves with a film of sparkles," said Mother Nature.

"Why do leaves turn colors in the fall?" asked Raggedy Ann, who'd been meaning to ask that question for a long time. And who better to ask than Mother Nature?

"Because when the ground begins to get hard and cold, a tree's trunk needs to save all the moisture it can possibly squeeze out of the earth for itself; there isn't enough to go around and share with all the thousands of leaves on its branches, especially since leaves evaporate their moisture into the air. Without moisture, the leaves dry up, turn those beautiful autumn colors, and drift to the ground. They've done their job of manufacturing food for the tree, and next year new ones will take their places when the spring rains and sunshine melt the earth," explained Mother Nature.

"Now, the pine needles on my *evergreen* trees and bushes— that's another story. Those needles are much skinnier than leaves, so they need less moisture, and each needle is covered with a waxy coating that keeps the moisture from evaporating away. That's why they stay green and remain on the branches right through winter."

"But how do all the other leaves know when the time has

come to change colors and fall off the branches?" asked Raggedy Andy.

"They listen for the call of the wind," answered Mother Nature. "It goes something like this:

> 'Come, Little Leaves,' says the wind one day,
> 'Over the meadow with me to play.
> 'Put on your dresses of red and gold.
> 'Summer is gone, and the days grow cold.'
>
> Soon as the leaves hear the wind's loud call,
> Down they come fluttering, one and all.
> Then, fast asleep in their earthy beds,
> The snow lays a coverlet over their heads.

"I like the wind's song," said Raggedy Ann, bending down to pick up a gold leaf that had fallen at her feet. "But it's a pity such lovely leaves are just wasted on the ground."

"Nothing goes to waste in my woods," said Mother Nature. "Sit down and I'll tell you what Mother Earth once told me.

"There was a time when the earth was covered with only rock and water—nothing was growing anywhere, because there wasn't any soil. But gradually, over millions of years, the rock covering began to crack into smaller pieces, and these in turn were ground into even smaller pieces by glaciers, which are huge moving mountains of ice, and by water and wind. Soon tiny things began to grow in the cracks between the pieces of rock. When they died, they decayed and got mixed in with the bits and chunks of crumbled rock, and slowly this crumbly mixture got thicker and softer as more and more things grew

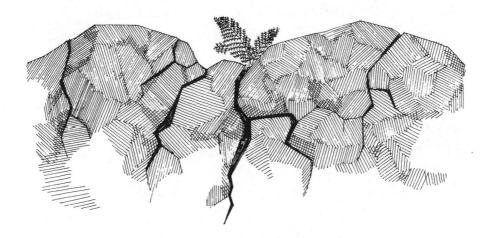

in it and died in it. And the more things grew and died, the richer the soil became, so that still more trees and flowers could grow. Soon much of the earth was covered with a soft carpet of soil, with green forests and fields of flowers growing where there had once been only rock.

"When the leaves fall to the ground," continued Mother Nature, "they give back to the soil many of the good nourishing things they borrowed from it while they were growing, and that helps the soil nourish new trees and new leaves. You Raggedys can help too, you know," said Mother Nature.

"How?" asked Raggedy Ann. "There are no leaves falling off me!"

"By putting back into the soil the remains of living things— not only leaves, but grass cuttings from the lawn mower, twigs, flower stems, even what's left over from the things we eat: tea leaves, coffee grounds, apple skins, old lettuce leaves, carrot tops, orange peels, anything that is part of something that was once alive. We call these remains *organic matter,* which includes the dead mouse Marcella buried last spring, bird droppings and any kind of animal manure. When organic matter decomposes back into the soil, it fills the soil with the nourishing things that new plants need to grow.

"But that isn't all it does," added Mother Nature. "It also makes the soil the right *texture*. In order for plants to grow healthy, they need soil that doesn't stay muddy for too long after it rains or the roots and bulbs will drown. They also need soil that doesn't bake dry and hard as a rock when the hot summer sun comes out. Soil that has too much *clay* in it will do both these things—one day it will be like a mud puddle and the next day it will be like cement. If we can add decaying organic matter to it, and rake it in, the soil will be much better for growing things.

"The opposite kind of soil is too *sandy*," Mother Nature went on to explain. "The water drains away so fast the flowers don't get a chance to take their drink—just like water does when you pour it into a hole you've dug on the beach. And the water washes away the nourishing minerals so the plants don't get enough to eat. If we can add organic matter to this kind of soil, it will hold moisture a little longer, and replace the plant food that was washed away.

"The third kind of soil is just right," laughed Mother Nature, remembering the story of Goldilocks and the Three Bears. "It isn't too sandy, and it doesn't have too much clay. It is called *loam*, and that means there is just enough clay in it to hold moisture, just enough sand in it to keep it loose and crumbly, and enough organic matter in it to be full of good food. Loam will get even better, however, if you rake organic matter into it from time to time, so you see, all three kinds of soil are improved by the remains of living things. But first, those remains have to begin to decay."

"How do we help that happen?" asked Raggedy Ann, who wanted to be sure she contributed her share to the lovely things that grew in the deep, deep woods. "We might plant a little vegetable garden next spring, if someone shows us how, and we will need some organic matter to add to our garden soil."

"You can build your own supply of decaying organic matter by raking a bunch of my beautiful autumn leaves into a pile in a corner of Marcella's yard. (It won't be a very pretty pile, so pick a corner where it will hardly show.) This kind of pile is called a *compost* pile, or a compost heap, and that means the decaying matter is made up of only leaves and plants and vege-

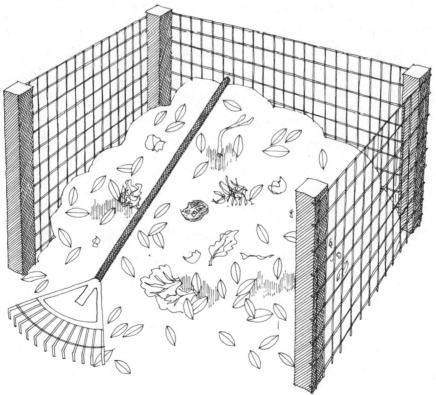

table remains. The reason you don't add animal remains to it is that neighborhood dogs and cats and mice and rats would come running right to it if you filled it with nice plump roast beef bones, or the tuna fish sandwich you didn't finish at lunch!"

"Fido would surely love that!" laughed Raggedy Ann, thinking about how much Marcella's dog appreciated a big fat bone, a little lean bone, or any bone at all that he could sink his teeth into.

"After you rake your leaves into a neat pile, you can start adding all sorts of vegetable leftovers from Marcella's kitchen, pushing them with your shovel into the center of the leaves. It's the inside part of the compost heap that decays the fastest—the dampness and the heat that builds up inside really speed the process on its way," said Mother Nature. "Be sure you make a little dent with your shovel in the leaves on the top of the heap, so the dent will catch the rain and your pile won't dry out.

"If you plant a garden next spring, you will probably buy a bag of fertilizer from Mr. Tubble's store, and your compost will decay even faster if you sprinkle some fertilizer on the pile now and then," she advised the Raggedys. "The only other thing to remember is to keep adding to your pile whenever you can— grass clippings, when the lawn is mowed, seaweed, if you live by the shore, and even branches from Marcella's Christmas tree. After a few months, you will see that the inside part of the pile is beginning to get soft and black. When it reaches that stage, we call it *humus,* but some folks call it gardener's gold!

"One last thing," added Mother Nature. "Ernie Earthworm loves compost as much as Fido loves bones! Earthworms help change compost into humus, so if you find him and his friends in your pile, you will know that you're really in luck!"

The two Raggedys thanked Mother Nature for telling them all about Mother Earth and her soil, and about how easy it would be to start a compost heap of their own. Then they ran home to get their rakes, and you know what happened? They not only learned something that day, but they also *earned* something as well: Mr. Tubble paid them each 50¢ for raking up the leaves around his store, and two gnomes who lived in a pretty house down the road not only donated all their leaves to the Raggedys' growing pile, but also invited them in for some sugar cookies and a glass of fresh fall cider.

Maybe you can work out an arrangement like that with some of *your* neighbors when you start to build your own compost heap!

CHAPTER FIVE

SANTA'S HELPERS

RAGGEDY ANDY had just come into the house, after adding some cabbage leaves from dinner to the center of his compost pile, and as he tried to scrape some damp leaves off his feet he thought he heard someone mumbling.

"Hmmmn," he heard. And "Uhmmn."

He looked around Marcella's room, but he couldn't see anyone moving or talking, so he thought maybe he'd been hearing things. But there it was again.

"Ahhh. Mmnn."

Now he could see who it was! There sat Raggedy Ann, pencil in hand, staring at a piece of paper. Every once in a while she would nod her head slightly and breathe a little sigh—like

69

people do when they are thinking very hard about something. Suddenly there was a ripping noise, and Raggedy Ann reached up and touched her head.

"That did it," she laughed. "I was thinking so hard I popped a stitch in my head!"

"What are you thinking about?" asked Raggedy Andy, who didn't like to be left out of plans and projects, especially the kind Raggedy Ann dreamed up.

"I'm thinking that Christmas is coming," said Raggedy Ann. "And I'd like to grow some presents for all our friends!"

"Well, isn't that what we're doing?" asked Raggedy Andy. "I mean, all those pots of bulbs we just put in the cellar—I thought those would be our gifts this year."

"But they won't be ready to bloom by Christmas time," Raggedy Ann reminded him. "Only the Paperwhites we planted in a gravy pitcher over there by Marcella's window, and maybe the dish of crocuses I planted for Mother Nature."

"Let's ask Annabel-Lee and Thomas," suggested Raggedy Andy. "They said they had many more secrets to tells us about indoor gardening."

So the two Raggedys tugged gently at Annabel-Lee's hat and explained what they wanted to know.

"Oh," said Annabel-Lee, "I thought you'd never ask! Thomas and I are so used to living in a city apartment that we know all kinds of things you can grow indoors, at any time of year, and they hardly cost anything at all to get started. We can make a whole garden out of things Marcella's parents have in the kitchen! All we need are some containers and some potting soil, and a bag of coarse sand."

"Mr. Tubble's store is closed. It's after six," said Raggedy

Andy. "I'm sure we can find all sorts of containers around the house, but—"

"I know!" Raggedy Ann interrupted. "I can *wish* for the packages of soil and sand with my magic wishing pebble!"

"Perfect!" said Thomas. "But how will we all get downstairs to the kitchen without anyone seeing us?"

"We'll wait 'til everyone's asleep, silly," answered Annabel-Lee, as if she were used to trotting upstairs and down in the middle of the night. "If anyone catches you, just say you're sleepwalking!"

That night, when everyone in Marcella's house was sound asleep, the dolls tiptoed past Marcella, and together they managed to push open the bedroom door. Very slowly, they made their way toward the stairs—especially Uncle Clem, who had gotten a new Scottish kilt to replace his worn one and didn't want to tear his new clothes by falling down the steps.

Inch by inch, they slid down the stairs on their stomachs, until they reached the bottom floor. Then, feeling their way along the wall, they finally felt the swinging door that led to the kitchen, and with a mighty shove, they were in!

"How will we get the light on?" asked Henny, the Dutch doll, who was so nervous, his one remaining wooden shoe was clattering like a jumping bean across the linoleum floor (his other shoe had become a home for a Roman hyacinth bulb, but he still had hopes of getting it back after the hyacinth finished blooming). "I can't even see my hand in front of my face!"

"I will climb up on Andy's shoulders," offered Raggedy Ann, "and Uncle Clem can climb on mine, and Thomas can climb on his, and that way we'll be able to reach the switch."

Five times they tried, and five times they fell. Then Annabel-

Lee suddenly thought of something. "If you open the refrigerator door, a light turns on—at least it did in our apartment in the city. Let's try it." She felt her way around the kitchen until she heard the soft sound of the refrigerator motor. Then she reached way up and grabbed the door handle and—Bingo!— the light went on and the dolls could see all the goodies inside.

"There," said Annabel-Lee, "I already see what we can use."

"First of all," she explained, "there are carrots. You cut off the green tops of several carrots, leaving about ½ inch of the vegetable still attached to the green tops, and stand them up in a shallow pot or a dish with ½ inch of sand in it. Water it well, and I bet in a week, new leaves will have started to grow on your green carrot 'trees'!"

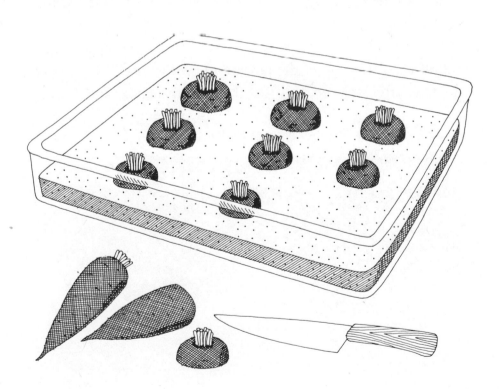

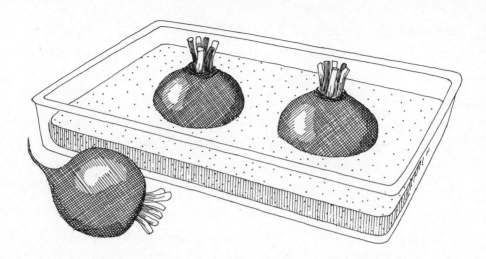

"You can do the same thing with beet tops, too," said
Thomas, pulling a bunch of beets out of the refrigerater bin,
"and the 'trees' they grow into have bigger leaves and reddish
stems."

"Oh, and look," said Annabel-Lee, "there's a pineapple! You
cut off the green top of the pineapple; with a small section of
the fruit still attached, pull off the bottom leaves, and let the

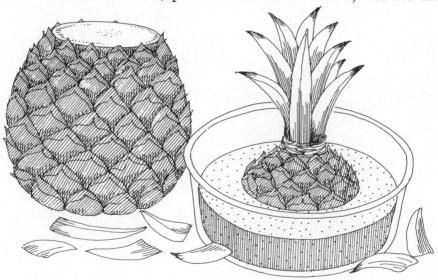

cut pineapple top dry for a day. Then stand it in a dish with about an inch of sand in it, water it well, put it near a bright but not too sunny window, and in a week or two it will grow new leaves on top. Soon it will get so big you will have to put it into a good-size flower pot! I have known some pineapple plants that even grew a new pineapple on top, but mostly, they just stay lovely big green plants."

"Remember," said Thomas, "that when you lift your new pineapple plant out of its dish and put it into a pot (after about six weeks), you must put some stones or broken pieces of flower pots over the drainage hole inside to keep the soil from packing down into the hole—just like you did when you potted your bulbs. And the soil you use should be loose and crumbly, so mix a bunch of sand in with some of the potting soil, the same way you did for the bulbs!"

"After the pineapple is growing in its pot, it likes plenty of sunshine," added Annabel-Lee, "because pineapples come from the islands of Hawaii, where the sun shines nearly every day."

"What's that funny-looking thing?" asked Raggedy Andy, pointing to something that looked like a shiny dark green pear.

"That's an avocado," said Thomas. "You can take out the big pit inside and grow it in water like you did with your hyacinth bulbs. Stick a few toothpicks around the pit near its flat bottom, and place it over the opening of a jar filled with water high enough to just touch the bottom of the seed. With the hyacinth bulb, the water was supposed to be not quite touching the base, but avocados like to dip their toes in a little!" he laughed.

"If you keep the water level in the jar just right for about a month or so, and place the jar in a warm but not too bright spot, you will see the roots begin to grow down into the bottom of the jar and then you will see a crack open up in the top of the seed," said Annabel-Lee. "Then a miracle will happen in front of your eyes! A green shoot will poke up out of the crack, and soon lovely green shiny leaves will appear! When the main stem is about 6 inches tall, snip off the top 3 inches of it so that the plant's energy won't all go into the job of making the main stem grow taller and taller, and it will use some of its energy to send out several side branches instead. This is called *pinching back*.

"A few weeks later, when the side branches are growing nicely and the roots look good, transfer it into a tallish flower pot filled with sandy soil, and give it plenty of moisture and sunshine. I've seen avocado plants grow taller than Marcella," laughed Annabel-Lee, "so every now and then when the roots poke out of the pot, you have to transfer it into an even bigger one!"

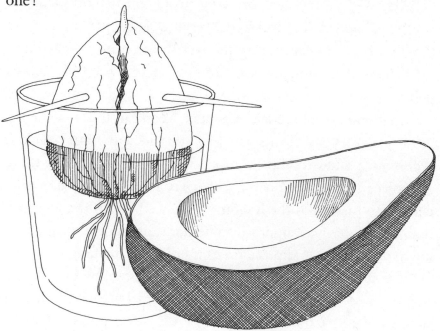

"I'm going to hunt around under the sink for some containers and old jars," said Raggedy Ann. "There might be some empty coffee cans we could use, or some cake tins, or some plastic containers—who knows what I'll find."

Raggedy Ann was in the middle of poking about under the sink when her hand felt something round with bumps on it. "What's this?" she asked, holding the object up for Annabel-Lee's inspection.

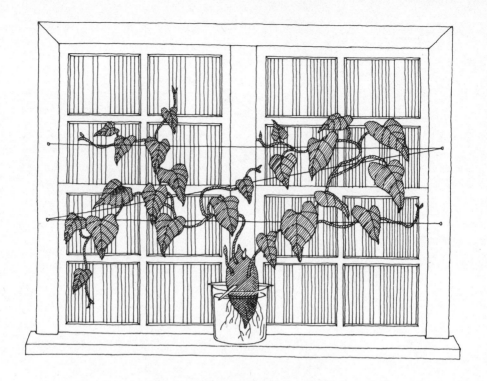

"A sweet potato!" said Annabel-Lee. "And it is as sweet to grow as it is to eat. You are lucky that it has those bumps. They are called the 'eyes' of the potato, and if a sweet potato doesn't have those 'eyes' it means it has been coated with wax to keep it fresh longer in the grocery store, and coated sweet potatoes won't grow. But this one is perfect—we can put it into a jar of water, just like an avocado, with the part of the potato that has eyes on it facing up. The beautiful sprouts that grow up from it will soon form a beautiful vine, which you can train to grow around a string or a wire that you stretch across a sunny window (vines love to climb, and will attach themselves to whatever is handy!). If you want to give it to someone as a present, you can transfer it to a pot of soil and leave the vine trailing out of it like ivy."

"Another thing you can do," said Thomas, "is make a little apple orchard out of apple seeds, or a little orange grove from orange seeds. Lemon and grapefruit seeds work too, but of course none of the trees will bear fruit—they'll just be lovely to look at! You wash and dry the seeds, put a few on the top of the soil you put into each of your containers (sandy soil is the easiest for seeds to grow in), cover them with just a little more soil and keep them moist and in a warm spot (but not directly in the sun) until they *germinate* (sprout). Then take a scissors and snip off all the seedlings except the strongest one in each pot, and move the pots into sunny parts of the house. Some will germinate in three weeks, but others take much longer, so don't grow impatient or forget to keep them moist!" finished Thomas.

"You also can grow many different kinds of seeds and plants in a *terrarium*," said Annabel-Lee. "A terrarium is a large glass

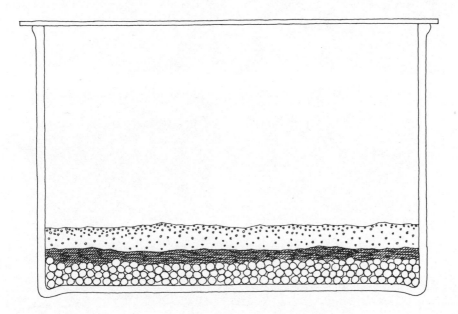

or plastic container that has a cover—a pane of glass you lay on top of it, or a sheet of clear plastic wrap. The cover keeps the moisture in the container so you only have to add a tiny bit of moisture once a month, and the air and soil in it will stay warm and damp. An aquarium will do nicely, or an old goldfish bowl, or even a large mayonnaise jar. Plant stores have all kinds of terrarium containers you can buy.

"When you've decided on your container," she continued, "you put about an inch of pebbles or aquarium gravel on the bottom of it for good drainage, cover the pebbles with a layer of dead leaves (or some charcoal chips you can get from the fireplace or a plant store), and add a layer of potting soil. Then you can sprinkle some seeds on the top of it, or bury the roots of a plant that is already growing—the woods are full of tiny pine tree seedlings and mosses and little sprigs of fern and ivy that you can dig up very carefully and transfer to the soil of your container. And catalogs and plant stores have all kinds of terrarium plants for sale, too."

"And you know what?" interrupted Thomas. "You can create a little landscape in your container by adding small statues of animals or a very small toy house. You can even put a piece of mirror in one spot to look like a pond, and sprinkle grass seed around it which will grow like a miniature meadow—of course you will have to mow the grass with your scissors from time to time!" he laughed.

"The next thing you do," said Annabel-Lee, "is to spray your terrarium garden with a fine spray—an empty window-cleaner bottle that you fill with water is perfect for the job. When you have finished planting it, you wipe off the sides of the container so it looks bright and clean, cover it but leave just a tiny open-

ing for air to get in, and set it in a showplace near a sunny window; don't give it too much full sunlight, or it will bake the plants inside!" she added.

"Then sit back and watch it grow and grow and grow—all you will ever have to do is trim the growing plants when they get too big for the bowl, and spray a tablespoon or two of water in it every four weeks," said Thomas.

"My goodness," said Raggedy Ann. "What will Marcella's parents think when they discover some of their fruits and vegetables have vanished in the night!"

"I'm sure they won't mind when they see all the beautiful plants growing around the house, but we can leave them a note:

A FEW THINGS ARE MISSING. WE BEG YOUR PARDON. THEY'VE DECIDED TO BECOME AN INDOOR GARDEN.

THANK YOU."

Then all the dolls pitched in to get the work done, and by the time they were finished, they had already missed half a night's sleep. They tiptoed out of the kitchen and climbed wearily back upstairs to dream of carrot trees and lemon groves and avocado plants. As they snuggled under their covers, Raggedy Andy said, "I'm so tired, I bet I will fall asleep before anyone else!"

But there wasn't one doll left awake to answer.

CHAPTER SIX

GRAMPY GROUNDHOG GETS A GARDEN

CHRISTMAS had turned out to be a great success, and many of the plants that had grown big enough to be given away as gifts were now thriving happily in the homes of the Raggedys' woodland friends. The pineapple plant looked quite handsome on Henrietta Hedgehog's window sill. Sophia Spider found her sweet potato vine a delight to climb on, and she liked to swing down from the tip of it on a silken thread. Charlie Chipmunk loved his forest of beet trees, and Mother Nature thought her dish of crocuses was as pretty and colorful as any she had ever grown herself.

And Marcella's parents thought the house looked lovely with all that greenery growing about, even though they didn't know who had planted it, or who could possibly have written that

note. "Maybe Fido is a magic dog," laughed Marcella's father, "or maybe he's a flower fairy in disguise!"

Fido knew, but he wouldn't tell.

Today was February 2nd, and the Raggedys thought they'd pay a visit to Tiny Town to wish everyone a Happy Groundhog Day.

"Let's visit Grampy Groundhog first," said Raggedy Ann. "He's been sleeping all winter and he is probably eager for some company, especially since today is Groundhog Day."

So the two Raggedys set out for Grampy Groundhog's house, and they were almost there when they met Ned Gnome scurrying in the opposite direction.

"Better stay clear of Grampy's house," he said. "Grampy is awful grumpy about the trouble between him and Percy Pig, and all he can do is sit in his rocking chair and cry."

"Then we'll certainly want to stop by and cheer him up," said Raggedy Ann. "But what has Percy Pig done to make Grampy so sad?"

"Grampy had just finished planting a nice garden in back of his house last spring when along came Percy Pig and rooted it all up! Little Percy Pig is almost always putting his snout into other people's business, and now Grampy is afraid to plan a new garden for fear that Percy will root it up again. I tell you, it's terrible to see a grown Groundhog cry!"

"Why don't *we* plant a garden for Grampy," said Raggedy Andy. "We'll plan it very carefully, we'll make it small enough so it won't be too much work, and Grampy can just sit back and watch it grow! And we'll see to it that Percy Pig never ruins it ever again."

"How will you do that?" asked Ned Gnome, knowing what a nuisance Percy could be when he had a mind to.

"We'll plant him a little garden all his own," laughed Raggedy Ann. "With seeds left over from the one we plant for

Grampy. But first we have to decide what kinds of things to plant—"

"Someone's coming," Raggedy Andy interrupted, for there definitely was someone moving toward them, and he was wearing a yellow velvet jacket, big buckle shoes, a snappy red bowtie and a beanie hat. "It's Grampy himself! Good day, Grampy."

> "Good day? Good Day? It's bleak and cold.
> I'd give all this snow for one marigold.
> Why, when I've tried to be honest and good,
> Was I cursed with a Pig in my neighborhood?
> Why have my tender carrots and beets,
> Accompanied Percy's salads and meats?
> Why did my spinach and lettuce greens,
> Leave my garden along with my beans?
>
> Oh, think of all the happy hours
> I used to spend with my zinnia flowers!"

"Don't cry, Grampy, we're going to plant you a whole new garden. We were just coming to tell you that, and to look through your seed catalogs so we can pick out the kinds that are easy to grow and fast to come up."

So the two Raggedys and Ned Gnome and Grampy Groundhog went indoors, got out paper and pencil, and began to look through Grampy's catalogs.

"We'll start with flowers," said Raggedy Ann. "Ned Gnome, since you won the first prize at last year's Tiny Town and Country Garden Contest, could you tell us the kinds of things we ought to know?"

"Delighted," said Ned Gnome, who was as nice as he was small. "There are two kinds of flowers, *annuals* and *perennials*. *Annuals* complete their entire life cycle in one growing season —they bloom the first year you plant them and then die. They never bloom again, so each year you have to plant new seeds, but they come up fast, so no one minds. *Perennials* take two years or longer to get to the flowering stage after you plant them, but then they keep coming again each year by themselves, sending out new stems from their old roots. So I guess you'd better plant only annuals in your first garden, or Grampy won't have the fun of seeing any flowers bloom in it this summer."

"The two annuals that I love best are zinnias and marigolds," said Grampy; "they bloom all through the summer until the frost sets in. They're easy, too—I used to let Georgie Groundhog plant them for me when he was a little fellow." Thinking about those good old days, he began to cry again.

"Sunflowers are a good choice as well," said Ned Gnome. "They're annuals, they grow like crazy, and you can feed the seeds that grow on their big faces to the birds. Or you can crack the seeds open and eat the little nut inside—absolutely delicious!" said Ned Gnome.

"I love them myself," snuffled Grampy Groundhog.

"Good, then it's settled," said Raggedy Ann. "We'll plant marigolds and zinnias and sunflowers. It says in this catalog that there are dwarf kinds of marigolds and zinnias, which are short, and tall kinds of them as well. We could—"

"Plant a row of dwarf marigolds in front of a row of taller ones," suggested Raggedy Andy.

"Or we could plant a row of giant zinnias with a little row of short ones on each side," said Raggedy Ann.

"Or we could plant giant zinnias with dwarf marigolds in front," said Andy.

"But I want some vegetables too," said Grampy. "I mean I *am* a vegetarian, you know."

"Of course," said Raggedy Ann. "But I can see how boys and girls might want to plant just zinnias of different heights, or just short and tall marigolds (short ones are usually called French marigolds, and tall ones are called African marigolds), for the fun of comparing them side by side—like Granny Field-mouse suggested we do with the different kinds of tulips some year."

"Now let's pick some easy-to-grow vegetables," said Raggedy Andy, turning to a different section of the seed catalog.

"How about beets?" he asked.

"Beautiful," said Grampy.

"Carrots?"

"Colossal."

"Lettuce?"

"Let us."

"Radishes?"

"Ravishing."

"Spinach?"

"Splendid."

"String beans?"

"Stupendous."

"Tomatoes?"

"Terrific."

"It's a good thing you are at the end of the alphabet," said Ned Gnome; "otherwise you'd need a football field for your garden!"

"Lots of boys and girls wouldn't want to plant all those different vegetables," said Raggedy Ann. "They might do very well with just a few rows of lettuce and carrots and radishes and beets. Those are the ones you plant early in spring, when the ground has thawed out, and since they grow fast and are picked fast, the garden will probably be over by the time school is out and the sun is hot. That way, a person can have the fun of gardening in the spring, without the bother of tending to it in the summer!"

"But I like those other vegetables," protested Grampy. "Wouldn't have a garden without them."

"What varieties should we order?" asked Raggedy Andy.

"It doesn't matter that much," said Ned Gnome. "But I have found these to be quite tasty and easy to grow: Crosby Early Egyptian beets; Red Cored Chantenay carrots; Salad Bowl lettuce is the prettiest kind I've ever seen, but any kind with *loose* leaves is good—Boston, Black Seeded Simpson, Ruby (which is red!); Bountiful Bush snap beans (or any kind of Bush snap beans you can get); New Zealand spinach; Scarlet Globe radishes; Marglobe or Rutgers tomatoes.

"Now here are some other things you should know," Ned

Gnome continued. "Tomatoes take a long time to get started, so if you want to plant some in your first garden, you should get a young tomato *seedling* (a plant that has already started growing) from your plant store, and transplant it into a spot in your garden as soon as the nights have become *warm* enough so your seedling won't catch cold!

"Some plants," explained Ned, "can't take cool weather, like the tomato, and so you have to wait and not plant them until the last frost is gone from where you live. Aside from the tomato, this includes the string beans, the New Zealand spinach, the marigolds, the zinnias and the sunflowers. If you plant these seeds too early in spring, you will be very disappointed."

"I promise to wait until it's warm," laughed Raggedy Ann, who was writing little notes all over her list as fast as her rag hand could manage.

After making their list, the Raggedys had to decide just where in Grampy's yard the garden should go, and how big it should be. They went outside to look around.

"I don't think we should put it where Grampy's garden used to be," said Raggedy Andy thoughtfully. "There's a tree too near it, and it blocks out some of the sun. Its roots are too close to it, too—the roots would rob our plants of the food in the soil, and no little plants of mine are going to go hungry if I can help it!"

"How about over there by Grampy's fence?" asked Raggedy Ann.

"A fence next to a garden is nice," said Ned Gnome. "But the puddle in that place shows that the soil has too much clay in it, and your little seedlings would do better in sandier soil than that."

Finally they found a perfect spot—lots of sun, no trees too near, no puddles, good crumbly soil, and close enough to Grampy's house so that Grampy could keep an eye on how everything was growing.

Now the Raggedys had to figure out what size it should be. "I think it should be small enough so that we can bend over and reach any spot in the entire garden while standing *outside* the border. That way, when we are working on the garden, we won't have to worry that we might be trampling on tiny seedlings by accident."

"Let's see," said Raggedy Andy. "We could make it 3 feet by 8 feet, and plant the rows the short way, across it, or we could make it a 5-foot square."

"Five feet on each side sounds good to me," said Raggedy Ann. "Next year, if we really like gardening, we can make a much bigger one, with wider rows. But this year, small is best!"

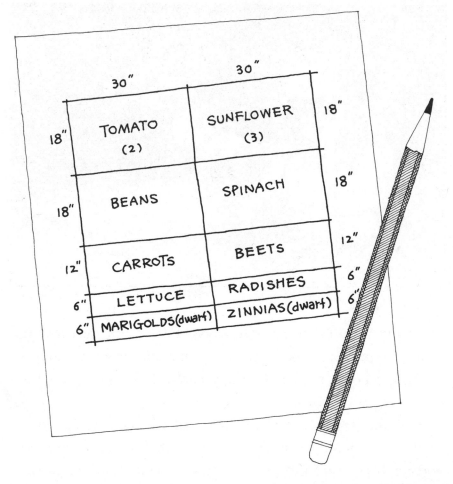

"You could consider this a sample garden," said Ned Gnome. "And plant just a few of each kind on your list. The ones you like most after you see how they all grow this year can be planted in much greater number next year, and the ones you end up liking least can be omitted altogether. If you divide each row of your small garden in half, you can even get two different kinds in each row."

Raggedy Ann took a piece of paper and drew a plan of what the garden would look like. She made a square box on the page,

5 inches on each side (each inch would equal one foot in the real garden), and divided it down the center with a line. Then she drew lines across the box to represent each row, allowing fatter rows for the plants like the Bush snap beans, the tomatoes, and the sunflowers, and skinnier rows for the small plants, like radishes and carrots. She put the fatter rows on the side of the garden facing north, so that the taller plants which grew there wouldn't cast a shadow over the shorter plants in the other rows and block out their share of the sunshine in the mornings and early afternoon (in North America, the sun shines down from a southerly direction, so things planted on the northern side of the garden won't interfere with the sun's rays).

When the plan was finished, she marked along the side of each row the number of inches wide the row would actually be in Grampy's garden, and labeled each row with the name of the plant that should go in it. She only had enough room for two tomato plants, three sunflowers, and several string bean bushes, and since she had used up the fat rows for those plants, she saw there wouldn't be room for giant zinnias and African marigolds, which also take a lot of space.

"Well," said Raggedy Andy, "we can just plant dwarf zinnias and French marigolds in the skinny row in front—they will make a bright border, and next year we will plant the other ones. We can't fit *everything* in!"

This is what their plan looked like:

"That's a good first garden," said Ned Gnome, who has supervised many a garden in his day. "Those who don't like spinach can plant more lettuce there instead. By planting lettuce two weeks later than they did in the first row, they will have some extra lettuce to eat after they have finished the heads from the first row. Or they could use that spot for growing herbs—chives, basil, dill, or mint."

"I've got another idea," suggested Grampy Groundhog.

"When the radishes are all eaten, we can use that row for planting pansies that we buy already started and ready to bloom at the flower store. You pull the little pansy plant and its soil right out of the tiny container it comes in, dig a hole for it in the row, and plunk it into the ground, soil and all. If you pick each flower off as it dies, the plant will develop new ones, and they will bloom and bloom all summer!"

As you can see, they all had ideas of their own to contribute, and if any of you want to plan a first garden, you can use the Raggedys' design or change it to suit your own idea of what a garden should grow. Just keep in mind the size of the plants when fully grown so there will be enough space for them in the row, and remember that taller plants should be on the north side of the shorter ones and the whole plot should be small enough to handle or you'll be working in your garden when you'd rather be off having fun.

"Well," said Grampy Groundhog, "this has turned out to be a fine Groundhog Day after all, and you know that a good Groundhog Day means spring is practically on the way!"

But it was a bit too soon to say that! On the way home, the

Raggedys found themselves in the middle of a snow storm, and *wooosh!* there went Raggedy Ann into a deep pile of snow. Raggedy Andy pulled on her foot, Ned Gnome pulled on Andy, but the two of them were too light to budge Raggedy Ann loose from under the snow. Just as they were giving up and Andy was going to call for help, Marcella came riding by on her sled and saw Raggedy Ann's foot sticking out.

"What are you doing way out here?" asked Marcella in surprise. "And what is this odd drawing in your apron pocket? Sometimes I think you dolls must have a hidden pair of wings," she laughed, "for you certainly seem to have more adventures than any real people I know. I made up a little poem about you this afternoon, when I looked all over the house and couldn't find you anywhere:

> I never know,
> From day to day,
> If you're going to be
> Where I put you away.
>
> I know you can't speak,
> I know you can't walk,
> But I bet you'd say plenty
> If rag dolls could talk!"

The Raggedys just looked at Marcella with their shoe-button eyes and their cheerful grins, and got a wonderful ride home through the snow on Marcella's sled.

CHAPTER SEVEN

SPRING FEVER!

MARCH 21ST! It was the first day of spring and Raggedy Ann woke up so excited about getting started on Grampy Groundhog's garden that she could barely lie still while she waited for Marcella to get ready and off for school. Then, with a merry leap from under her quilt, she was out of bed and standing next to Raggedy Andy's side.

"We'd better get our tools from the shed and get going," said Raggedy Ann. "We've got lots of work to do today if we want the soil to be all ready for planting by next week!"

So the two Raggedys climbed up and over Marcella's window sill and soon were on the path leading into the deep, deep woods. The whole path was bordered by drifts of daffodils getting ready to bloom. Here and there a few were already in

flower, and every time Raggedy Ann saw a daffodil's big yellow
trumpet, she squealed, "Look what's happening!" as if she
couldn't believe her eyes. The little bulb flowers—the snowdrops and crocuses and scilla—which the Raggedys planted in
Marcella's yard last autumn had started blooming over a month
ago, and the Raggedys thought their bright little faces were
more beautiful than anything they had ever seen before.

"I bet the Easter Bunny had plenty of warning *this* spring,"
laughed Raggedy Andy, looking around at all the glowing
flowers that had sprouted from the bulbs they had buried, bulbs
that would send up flowers for many more springs yet to come.

Soon they came to Mr. Tubble's store. "What can I do for
you this first day of spring?" inquired Mr. Tubble.

"We are going to need some good garden fertilizer to rake
into Grampy Groundhog's new garden, but we don't want very
much of it, and we don't know what kind to buy," said Raggedy Andy.

"Your choice should have three kinds of plant food in it," explained Mr. Tubble. "*Nitrogen,* for growing green leaves and stems; *phosphorus,* for strong roots, flowers and fruit; *potassium,* for good health, especially for roots—carrots and radishes and beets eat it up!"

"What do the numbers on these different bags of fertilizer mean?" asked Raggedy Ann.

"The first number," answered Mr. Tubble, "always stands for the percentage of nitrogen in the bag, the second stands for the amount of phosphorus, the third number stands for potassium. If you are growing only grass, like a lawn, you want a fertilizer that is high in nitrogen, because you are only concerned with stems and leaves, so you look for a bag that says

20-10-10. But for a flower and vegetable garden, you worry about good flowers and roots and fruit, not only leaves and stems. You want one in which there is at least as much phosphorus and potassium as there is nitrogen, and the percentage of phosphorus should really be greater than either of the other two foods. So I'll give you a bag of fertilizer marked 5-10-5.

"You will also need some other things, like four stakes to mark out the four corners of your little garden, and some good garden string to tie from one stake to another to show exactly where the four sides of your garden lie. And you will need some smaller stakes to mark the rows. If you stretch a length of string across the garden soil between the two stakes that mark every row, you will know exactly where the furrow should be made—all along the length of string.

"Speaking of seeds, what kinds would you like?" asked Mr. Tubble.

"Here's our list," said Raggedy Ann. "We looked through a seed catalog and decided on these. Next year we may order directly from a seed company, but this year we feel better getting them from you!"

"That's because I give you free advice!" laughed Mr. Tubble, as he went into the back room of his store to get some supplies. He came back carrying an old laundry basket in which he put a small bag of fertilizer, some garden twine, a bunch of little garden stakes and four bigger ones, and the little packets of seeds they had asked for.

"Here is a handy way to carry all the small things you need," he said. "Put your hand cultivator and your trowel in there too, and scissors to cut the string with. Add a pencil and some empty envelopes for extra seeds you want to save, and you will be all

set. You can each grab one handle of the basket with one hand and carry the shovel or hoe in the other. Good luck!"

Now the Raggedys were really excited! They felt just like professional gardeners, but they hoped Ned Gnome would be waiting at Grampy's house as promised.

When they got there, Ned Gnome was telling Grampy how beautiful the deep, deep woods looked this spring with all the daffodils and tulips coming up. "You're lucky to have the Raggedys planting your garden for you this year," he said to Grampy. "Each of them seems to have a green thumb."

"Nonsense," said Grampy. "They have tan thumbs—just like the rest of their hands."

"That's not what I meant," explained Ned Gnome. "A person who is good at growing things is said to have a 'green thumb,' and the Raggedys have done a fine job so far."

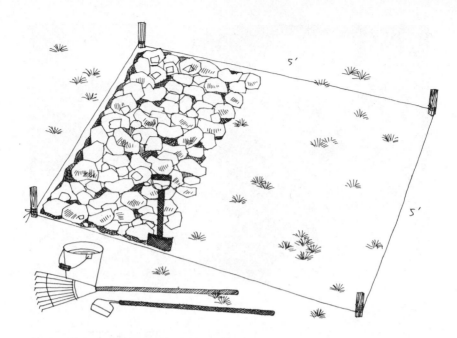

Soon the Raggedys and Ned Gnome were measuring out the garden, 5 feet on each side, and pounding in the corner stakes. Then Ned said, "Starting on one side and working toward the other, you Raggedys dig the earth up in chunks with your spade about 8 inches deep, and then chop up the chunks with your hoe. When that's done, rake through it to get rid of the stones and twigs and roots. When you've raked it nice and smooth, cover it over with a layer of compost from the center of your compost pile. Sprinkle some handfuls of fertilizer evenly from corner to corner, and rake it all into the soil. (In autumn, after your garden has finished growing and your vegetables have been eaten, you rake it clean and smooth again and cover it over with another layer of compost to put back into the soil what your growing plants will have taken out.) Give it a good watering, let it sit for a week or so, and you're ready to plant your seeds!" finished Ned.

"Easier said than done, I'll bet," laughed Raggedy Andy, and they got right down to business. It's a good thing the Raggedys had decided on such a small garden, because digging and hoeing and raking proved to be very hard work. They took turns: one would dig while the other used the hoe, then they'd change tools. In between, they had plenty of lemonade to sustain them, and they even took a rest for an hour lying on their backs and gazing at the different shapes the clouds made as they slowly drifted overhead.

"If I had real hands instead of rag ones, I'd surely have blisters by now!" said Raggedy Ann, as they cleaned the dirt off their tools. "I hope Marcella gives us another bubble bath when we get home."

All the following week, the Raggedys could think of nothing else but their garden, and finally the day came to sow the cool-season seeds.

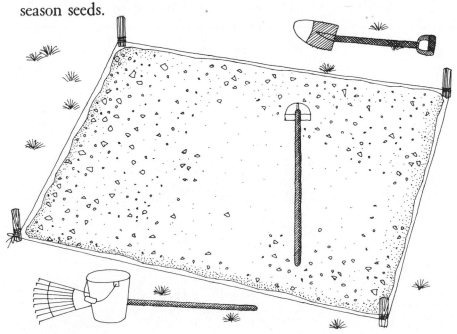

After they had divided the plot down the center with a string and fastened it to a small stake on either end, they began to measure out the rows across the garden, tying twine between each set of stakes. Then, with a pencil, they made a slim furrow along the length of the second row's line (the first row of marigolds and zinnias would be planted a few weeks later, when the weather was warmer), and dropped some of the very tiny lettuce seeds into the furrow on one half of the row.

They tried to space the seeds thinly and evenly apart according to the directions on the back of the packet, and with their hands they covered the seeds gently with soil and patted it firmly into place over the seeds. (Tiny seeds stick together, but you do the best you can; bigger seeds are no problem to space thinly.) Then they did the same with the radish seeds on the other half of the row, always making sure to follow the directions on the back of the packet, and watered the whole row

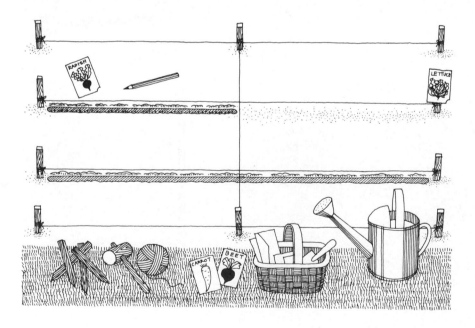

gently with their watering can because Ned Gnome had explained that seeds must be kept moist (but not drowned!) the whole time you are waiting for them to first sprout.

Raggedy Ann emptied the rest of the lettuce seeds into a blank envelope, and wrote the name of the seeds on the front of it, along with the depth they should be planted, and put the original (empty) seed packet over the stake on the lettuce side of the row. This whole routine was repeated for the radishes, and the next row of carrots and beets, and when they were finished, the garden looked like this:

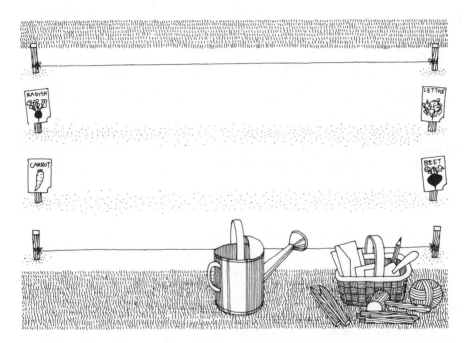

Several weeks later, when all the yellow daffodils had burst into flower in the deep, deep woods, and some spectacular red tulips were enjoying their finest hour in Marcella's yard, the Raggedys finished planting their garden with the warm-season

plants. The New Zealand spinach has tough seeds, so the Raggedys had soaked them in a glass of water for two days and
now they planted 14 seeds, each about 2 inches apart, in the
spinach spot. Next, the Bush snap beans went in, about 1½
inches apart, and then they planted about 5 sunflower seeds as
far apart from each other as the space would allow.

Raggedy Ann was working on the front row, planting her
marigold seeds, and Raggedy Andy was planting the zinnia
seeds in the other half of the row, when Ned Gnome arrived
with two tomato seedlings and showed the Raggedys how to
transplant them.

"Put your hand over the top of the pot with the little seedling stem between two fingers, tap the side of the pot against
something hard until you feel the whole lump of soil inside begin to give, and lift it out. Put water in the hole where it's going to go, before you lower it in, and set it a few inches deeper
than it was in the pot. See how easily it slips out?" he asked.

Raggedy Andy wanted to know: "How come you waited so late in the day to plant it?"

"Because if you plant it in the middle of the day, the strong sun can wilt it before it's adjusted to its new home," said Ned.

"Don't we need to tie them to stakes to help support the stems as they grow?" asked Raggedy Ann.

"I've got a broken broom handle I was saving for an occasion," said Grampy Groundhog, dashing into his house. He returned with some twistems (the kind that come with plastic bags), made a loose loop around each seedling stem with one twistem, and wound the ends of the twistem tightly around the stakes which he set into the ground about 3 inches away from each plant.

Raggedy Ann and Raggedy Andy had already learned something about *thinning* plants during the weeks which immedi-

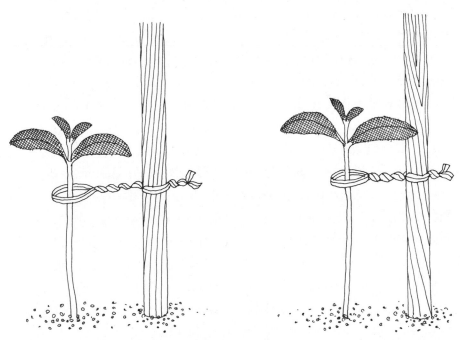

ately followed the planting of their cool-season vegetables. They had been shown by Ned how the new seedlings first send up two tiny leaves to feed the baby plant as it gets underway, but that soon a second pair of leaves appear which are called the "true" leaves. When this happens, it is time to *thin* the plants out in that row so there will be plenty of space and food and nourishment for the seedlings that remain in the row. The reason you don't plant the *seeds* that far apart in the first place, and save yourself all the trouble of thinning the seedlings out later, is that some seeds don't *germinate* (sprout) at all: if you only planted ten seeds to begin with in a row big enough for ten grown-up plants, you might end up with just three or four mighty lonesome plants! So it's better to start off by planting more seeds in the row and then take some out later to make enough room between the growing plants.

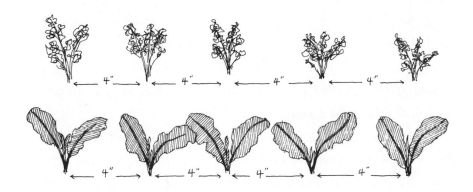

The distance apart has to do with the final size of the particular plant—radishes need only 1 or 2 inches of space between them as they grow, carrots and beets about 4 inches, lettuce about 8 inches, sunflowers at least 1 foot. The back of the packet usually tells how much to thin out the plants.

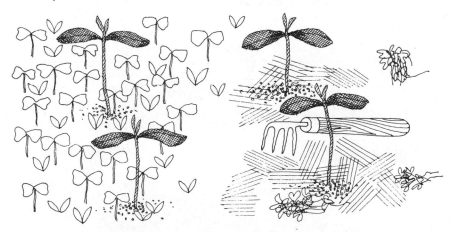

The other thing the Raggedys had learned about is called *cultivating* the garden—pulling up anything you find growing there that shouldn't be, and scratching the soil lightly around the plants with a fork or your hand cultivator to keep it loose and crumbly instead of hard or packed down. This only needs to be done about once a week, before you give your garden a long deep watering with a hose (don't water a few times a week lightly—that only makes the roots grow *up* to reach the moisture, instead of *down* where they belong). Of course, if the garden dries out before it's time to be watered, be sure to water it thoroughly right away.

Now Ned Gnome said he'd tell them a few other tricks. "Remember what Annabel-Lee and Thomas taught you about *pinching back* the main avocado stem so side shoots would grow? Well, do the same service for zinnias and marigolds when they are about 6 inches tall. But you should do the opposite for my tomato seedlings," he laughed, "because we don't want side shoots—we want to encourage one strong, tall main stem. So *pinch off* the new shoots as they appear in the places where a leaf joins the main stem."

"It's strange to think you can control the shape of plants by pinching back the main stem, or pinching off the side stems," observed Raggedy Ann. "I mean, you don't go around trying to make people taller by pinching off their arms, or make them grow fatter by pinching back their head!" she laughed.

Just then Laurie Ladybug lit on Raggedy Ann's apron. "What good luck!" said Ned Gnome. "Laurie Ladybug gets rid of insects for you that would like to get rid of your plants, and she's not the only friend who will help you keep your garden healthy and strong. Freddy Firefly, Ernie Earthworm, and the beautiful green praying mantis (what *is* his name? I don't often see him around these days) will all do their share."

"*Shhhhsh,*" said Laurie Ladybug. "The sun is so warm, and your voice is so soft, and the Raggedys are so tired from all their gardening, that they have fallen asleep while you were talking. I'm sure they didn't mean to be rude," soothed Laurie Ladybug, for Ned Gnome had a very sensitive nature.

"All work and no play makes Ned a dull gnome," laughed Ned. "I think I'll rejoin some of my friends—I hear them now."

117

WORTH
GRUELLE

When Raggedy Ann woke up, she gazed about her everywhere and rubbed her shoe-button eyes. The flowers looked more colorful in the woodland meadow than they had ever looked before. Even the grass was such a vivid green that it seemed to shimmer, and the sunbeams from the setting sun shone like beams of reddish gold. But best of all were the lovely, dainty fairyland creatures playing among the blades of grass and flying around the flowers.

"Isn't it beautiful, Raggedy Andy?" Raggedy Ann whispered.

"Indeed it is," Raggedy Andy replied.

The two Raggedys could now see that all the little fairies and elves and gnomes were playing a game—it was Frisbee! And the Frisbee was Raggedy Andy's little blue cap! The two rag dolls laughed and shouted and ran after the fairies as fast as their rag legs would carry them, but of course they could not run as quickly as the fairies could fly.

My, what great fun they had. Sometimes the little fairies would let the dolls get so close, the Raggedys could almost reach Raggedy Andy's hat. Then with a merry laugh the fairies would whisk the cap high up in the air, until finally one of the elves brought it back and placed it on Raggedy Andy's head.

Then they disappeared and all was quiet in the deep, deep woods, except for the ringing sound of spring peepers chirping on the pond far away.

"I must have been dreaming," said Raggedy Andy.

"Not dreaming," said Raggedy Ann. "We must have Spring Fever!"